3 ELA
Common Core

Dear Student,

Welcome to American Book Company's Common Core series! This series has been made just for you! Every book will give you practice for 100 percent of the common core standards. We have tried to explain each standard as clearly and simply as possible.

Our writers have also included Depth of Knowledge (DOK) levels in these books. You will see the levels in the chapters and the practice questions. These leveled questions will increase your ability to understand new concepts.

Also, with each grade 3–12 series, we have included free online testing from now until August 2014. If you have one of these books, the link and code are listed at the bottom of this page.

Using the code, go online and take the pretest. This is a tool you can use to find out which skills you already know. You can also determine which skills will need more work. When you finish the test, print out the results. Then give them to your teacher.

After you are done, you can use the book in different ways. You can work through all of the material in the book, paying close attention to the areas where you made mistakes. Or, if you do not have much time, you can only work on the parts where you made the most mistakes.

The online post test will also help you just like the pretest does. But, you should only take it after you finish the practices in the book.

If you are using the K–2 series, enjoy! Each book has many activities made just for you! There are also a lot of pictures and extra space for writing in your answers.

We look forward to hearing of your success as you master the Common Core standards!

Sincerely,

Frank J. Pintozzi

Dr. Frank Pintozzi
Executive Vice President
American Book Company
www.americanbookcompany.com
888-264-5877

Scan this QR code with your smart device to jump to the online testing page.

To access your pretest and post test, **visit americanbookcompany.com/online-testing/test.php** and select "**3rd Grade ELA CCS Pretest**" or "**Post Test.**" Enter the password "**sentence**" to access these tests.

Mastering the Common Core in Grade 3 English Language Arts

Author and Project Coordinator: Zuzana Urbanek

Contributing Writer and Reviewer: Tiffany N. Fick

Executive Editor: Dr. Frank Pintozzi

American Book Company
PO Box 2638
Woodstock, GA 30188-1383
Toll Free: 1 (888) 264-5877 Phone: (770) 928-2834
Toll Free Fax: 1 (866) 827-3240
Website: www.americanbookcompany.com

ACKNOWLEDGEMENTS

The authors would like to gratefully acknowledge the technical contributions of Marsha Torrens and Becky Wright.

We also want to thank Mary Stoddard and Charisse Johnson for their expertise in developing many of the graphics for this book.

PO Box 2638
Woodstock, GA 30188-1318

Printed in the United States of America

12/11 01/13

Table of Contents

Preface

Mastering the Common Core in Grade 3 English Language Arts will help students who are learning or reviewing the Common Core State Standards. The materials in this book are based on the Common Core standards and the model content frameworks as published by the Partnership for Assessment of Readiness for College and Careers (PARCC) consortium.

This book contains several sections:

1) General information about the book

2) A literature unit (chapters 2–3) with a Literature Review practice chapter

3) An informational texts unit (chapters 4–5) with an Informational Texts Review practice chapter

4) Seven additional chapters that review the concepts and skills and provide further practice

Standards are posted at the beginning of each chapter and at the beginning of each practice.

Teachers: See the "Answer Key and Teacher Resources for *Mastering the Common Core in Grade 3 English Language Arts*" to read tips for using this book and access additional material for classroom and one-on-one use.

We welcome comments and suggestions about the book. Please contact the authors at

American Book Company
PO Box 2638
Woodstock, GA 30188-1383

Toll Free: 1 (888) 264-5877
Phone: (770) 928-2834
Fax: (770) 928-7483
Website: www.americanbookcompany.com

About the Author and Project Coordinator:

Zuzana Urbanek is a professional writer and editor with over twenty-five years of experience in education, business, and publishing. She has taught a variety of English courses at the college level and also has taught English as a foreign language abroad. Her master's degree is from Arizona State University.

About the Contributing Writer and Reviewer:

Tiffany N. Fick completed her bachelor of arts degree in English Education at Indiana University. She is an elementary teacher in Atlanta Public Schools in Atlanta, Georgia, and also a Teach for America corps member. Although her concentration is in English language arts, she teaches all subjects, including science, social studies, reading, writing, and math.

About the Executive Editor:

Dr. Frank J. Pintozzi is a former professor of education at Kennesaw State University. For over twenty-eight years, he has taught English and reading at the high school and college levels as well as in teacher preparation courses in language arts and social studies. In addition to writing and editing state standard-specific texts for high school exit and end-of-course exams, he has edited and written several college textbooks.

Chart of Standards for *Mastering the Common Core in Grade 3 English Language Arts*

The following chart shows which Common Core Standards are covered in each chapter of this book. For a full list of Common Core Standards for grade 3, please see the Appendix.

Chapter	Common Core Standards Addressed
Chapter 1: How to Write Your Answers	(chapter about writing short and long responses; can pertain to any standard)
Literature Unit	
Chapter 2: Kinds of Literature	**RL** 1, 2, 4, 10, **RF** 4, **W** 1–5, 8, 10, **SL** 1.c–d, 2–4, **L** 5 (1–6 in writing tasks)
Chapter 3: Parts of a Story	**RL** 1, 2, 3, 5–7, 9–10, **RF** 4, **W** 1–5, 7, 10, **SL** 1.c–d, 2–4, **L** (1–6 in writing tasks)
Literature Review	**RL** 1–7, 9–10, **RF** 4, **W** 1–5, 7, 8, 10, **SL** 4, **L** (1–6 in writing tasks)
Informational Texts Unit	
Chapter 4: Informational Texts	**RI** 1, 2, 4, 6, 9, 10, **RF** 4, **W** 2, 4–8, 10, **SL** 1–3, **L** 1, 2, 3.a (1–6 in writing tasks)
Chapter 5: Understand What You Read	**RL** 7, 9, 10, **RI** 1, 3, 5, 7–10, **RF** 4, **W** 1, 2, 4–6, 8, 10, **SL** 4–6, **L** 1, 3, 6
Informational Texts Review	**RL** 7, 10, **RI** 1–10, **RF** 4, **W** 1, 2, 4–8, 10, **SL** 1–6, **L** 1–3, 6
Skills Review and Practice	
Chapter 6: Word Meaning	**RF** 3.c, 4.c, **L** 4–6
Chapter 7: Spelling	**RF** 3.a, b, d, **L** 4.b, c, d
Chapter 8: Parts of Speech	**W** 1.c, 2.c, 3.c **L** 1.a–i
Chapter 9: Conventions and Usage	**L** 2.a–d, 3.a, b
Chapter 10: Speaking and Listening	**SL** 1–6
Chapter 11: Research	**W** 7, 8, **SL** 1.a
Chapter 12: Writing	**W** 1–8, 10

Key

RL – Reading Literature	**W** – Writing
RI – Reading Informational Texts	**L** – Language
RF – Reading Foundational Skills	**SL** – Speaking and Listening

Reading Passages for Fluency

These passages are for you to read aloud to your teacher or tutor. He or she will tell you if you should read them aloud. You do not need to read them ahead of time.

Passage 1

Jabira

Jabira was so nervous about giving her book report in front of her class today. She knew she was nervous because she had butterflies in her stomach. She had practiced it in front of her mirror last night. She hoped she would remember what she wanted to say. When she got in front of the class, the other kids were not paying attention. Some were looking out the windows, and others were asleep at their desks. This made Jabira even more nervous. She began to talk, but her voice cracked. She cleared her throat so the kids would look at her.

Jabira started to speak, "My book report is on—" but was interrupted by some rude boys in the back yawning loudly and booing her. "Pay attention, class," Mr. Hampton ordered. He gave Jabira a smile. "Go on, Jabira."

Jabira coughed again and started over. She nervously shifted her weight on each foot. The class listened to her finish her report and even asked questions. When she was finished, Jabira returned to her seat. She smiled because she was so glad it was over.

Passage 2

Will Smith

Will Smith was born in 1968 in West Philadelphia. His mother, Caroline, was a school administrator. His father, Willard, was a refrigeration engineer. His parents separated when he was thirteen. Smith's charming and sly demeanor earned him the nickname "Prince." In 1985, while still in high school, Smith began making rap music with his friend Jeff Townes. Townes was a talented musician. They called themselves DJ Jazzy Jeff & the Fresh Prince. The group made humorous, radio-friendly songs like "Summertime." Their popularity grew quickly.

In 1989, their song "Parents Just Don't Understand" earned the first Grammy ever awarded for a hip-hop song. In 1990, NBC offered him the starring role in a new TV show. He accepted. The show, *The Fresh Prince of Bel-Air*, was a success. After excelling as a musician and TV star, Smith turned to making movies. He set himself the goal of becoming "the biggest movie star in the world." He starred in huge films like *I Am Legend* and *Men in Black*. His performance in *Ali* even earned him an Oscar nomination. By 2008, Will Smith felt he had fulfilled his goal.

Chapter 1
How to Write Your Answers

Welcome to *Mastering the Common Core in Grade 3 English Language Arts*! This book will help you review skills. It also will help you learn the standards for English language arts. You can use it to get ready for Common Core testing.

As you read this book, you will see practices. These have questions for you to answer. This is good practice for future tests. Many of the questions ask you to choose an answer from choices. You can choose answer A, answer B, answer C, or answer D. But some questions ask you to write an answer. This chapter will help you get ready to answer those questions that ask you to write.

Fill in the Blank

Some questions ask you to write your own answer. They will tell you to fill in the blank. Look at the sample passage below and questions that follow it. Both ask questions about the story.

The Grasshopper and the Ant

by Aesop

In a field one summer day, a Grasshopper was hopping about. He chirped and sang happily. An Ant passed by, carrying an ear of corn. With great toil, he dragged the corn toward his nest.

"Why not come and chat with me," said the Grasshopper, "instead of toiling in that way?"

"I am helping to lay up food for the winter," said the Ant. "I recommend you to do the same."

"Why bother about winter?" said the Grasshopper. "We have got plenty of food at present." But the Ant went on its way and continued its toil. The Grasshopper danced and sang.

> When the winter came, the Grasshopper found itself very hungry. He saw the ants every day, sharing the corn and grain they had collected in the summer.
>
> Then the Grasshopper knew ...
>
> It is best to prepare for the days of necessity.

While the Ant works, what does the Grasshopper do? List three things.

____

____

____

This question asks you to make a list. All you need to do is think about the character in the story. If you need to, look back at the story. Find the places where it tells what the grasshopper does. Then write down three things on the blank after the question. What did you write? You could write any of these: The grasshopper hops, chirps, sings, chats, and dances.

Longer Answers

At times, you will need to do more than fill in blanks or make lists. You may need to write a few sentences or a paragraph. Above all, be sure to answer the question clearly. Look at this example of a question about the same story.

What lesson can a reader learn from reading "The Grasshopper and the Ant"? Use facts from the story to support your answer.

____

____

This question is a little different. It asks for more than a word or two. You need to answer what it is asking. Again, look back at the story if you need to. Once you know the answer, think of how to say it. Use complete sentences. Tell what lesson you think the story teaches. For example, here is what Matt wrote. Look at how he uses part of the question in his answer.

> *A lesson readers can learn from the passage is that it is best to plan ahead. The grasshopper sees he was not smart. The ant planned for winter. The grasshopper did not, and now he is hungry.*

Notice how Matt used complete sentences. He also answered the question clearly. He said what the lesson was. He also used facts from the story to support his answer.

Writing Essays

You will also need to do some longer writing. These might be reports or essays. They might also be stories.

When you need to write an essay or story, you will see a prompt. A prompt is a description that tells you what to write about. It also might have some guidelines for what to include.

Before we look at **how to write your answers**, let's look at how they will be scored. When you take an actual test, trained readers will score what you write. Here are the score points they will most likely use. The chart of score points is called a **rubric**.

Rubric for 4-Point Scoring of Writing	
4 pts	The response shows that the student has a good understanding of the task. The student has provided a response that is accurate, complete, and answers the question. Support or examples are included. The writing is clearly based on the text.
3 pts	The response shows that the student has an understanding of the question. The response is accurate and answers the question. But support or details may not be complete or clear.
2 pts	The response shows that the student has some understanding of the concept. The response may be too general or too simple. Some of the support or examples may be incomplete or left out.
1 pt	The response shows that the student has very little understanding of the concept. The response is incomplete, has many mistakes, and might not answer the question.
0 pts	The response is not correct. It might be confused or not answer the question. Or the student does not respond at all.

You want to get the highest score you can when you write. Here are some ways to make sure you write the best responses.

Here are some steps to keep in mind when you need to write answers. These steps will help you write the best answers you can.

Read the Question Carefully

First of all, read the question carefully. Make sure you understand what it is asking. If you need help, ask your teacher.

Write Clearly

Answer each question in a clear way. If a question asks when something happened, be sure to talk about the sequence of events. If it asks you to compare two things, be sure to talk about how they are similar.

Being clear also means that your writing must be correct. Be sure to check your spelling. Also look for any other mistakes. If you find an error, erase it completely or cross it out. Write what you really wanted to say right above it or next to it.

Use Neat Handwriting

Make sure that people reading your answer can tell what it says. Write in a neat way that others can read.

Here is an example. Read the prompt carefully. Look at exactly what it asks you to do. Then, you will practice writing. You will also see what some other students wrote.

The Ugly Duckling

A mother duck waits for her ducklings to hatch. When the eggs crack, all of the babies look as she expects—except for one. He looks different from the others. Everyone on the farm thinks he is ugly and teases him. Finally, he runs away. But everywhere he goes, he is always teased because he looks different. He suffers for a long time. He spends a cold winter alone on a frozen pond. When spring comes, he sees some beautiful birds nearby. He is so lonely that he goes to them, expecting to be teased as usual. But the birds are friendly to him. Suddenly, he sees his reflection in the water. He realizes that he is not a duckling after all. He is a beautiful swan! He thinks that it was worth his suffering to be this happy.

Writing Task
Write a paragraph about the theme of this story. Use examples from the passage to support your idea. Use your own paper to write your response. Make sure your writing is clear and has a beginning, a middle, and an end.

What would your response be? Practice writing an essay that answers this prompt. Then, look at the sample responses from other students. Study how each one might score.

Model Student Response: 4-Point Score

The theme of "The Ugly Duckling" is that every person has to find a place in the world. Its hard to be different. The ugly duckling finds this out. Others push him around. He finds out he is not a duck at all, he is a swan! So he looked funny to other ducks but then blends in when he finds the swans. He figures it was okay to go thru all that to find where he really belonged.

Scoring Notes

This response would score 4 points. The student clearly answers the prompt about the theme of the story. The response begins by stating the theme, that "every person has to find a place in the world." The next five sentences supportthis idea. Examples are included of the ugly duckling's journey to find his place in the world. The details show that the student read the passage carefully and understood its meaning. There is a clear conclusion.

There are a few errors. In the second sentence, "Its" should be "It's." In the last sentence, "thru" should be spelled "through." There are also shifts in verb tense from present to past. However, these errors do not affect understanding.

Chapter 1

Model Student Response: 3-Point Score

> People are not nice if you look differnt. The charkter in the story was ugly. The farm animals tease him he runs away. Then he finds swans and sees he is one. They are friendly. becuz he looks like them. he is finaly happy.

Scoring Notes

This response would score 3 points. The student answers the prompt with a statement of a simple theme and support for this idea. The answer is not as complete as a 4-point response. It also has mistakes. Misspelled words include "differnt" (should be "different"), "charkter" (should be "character"), "becuz" (should be "because"), and "finaly" (should be "finally"). There should be no period after "friendly"—the sentence should read "They are friendly because he looks like them." In the last sentence, "he" should be capitalized. The mistakes do not prevent understanding.

Model Student Response: 2-Point Score

> The duckling was sad. He ran away. It was hard on him. Peeple shud not be mean. But the swans like him.

Scoring Notes

This response would score 2 points. The response shows some understanding of the question but is too general. It really does not talk about the theme of the story. It simply recounts events. However, the details included show that the student read and understood the passage. There are several mistakes even though the response is short. The writing switches between past and present tense. The word "Peeple" should be "People" and "shud" should be "should."

Model Student Response: 1-Point Score

> How come the mom duck dint luv her baby? so he was ugly. Not fair.

Scoring Notes

This response would score 1 point. This response does not answer the question in the prompt. It is not a complete paragraph. It uses only one detail from the passage. It also contains many mistakes. Only the first sentence is a complete sentence, and it has two misspelled words ("dint" should be "didn't" and "luv" should be "love").

Model Student Response: 0-Point Score

I do not know theme.

This response would score 0 points.

Chapter 1 Summary

You need to know how to write your answers. Some will be short answers that you write on a blank line. Others will be sentences or paragraphs.

A **4-point rubric** will be used to score your writing.

When you write answers, keep these points in mind:

- Read the question carefully.
- Write clearly.
- Use neat handwriting.

Chapter 1 Review

A.

DIRECTIONS **Now you can practice scoring. Read this passage and the prompt after it. Then read the answers that students wrote. Decide what score each answer should get. Discuss the score you gave with your teacher or tutor.**

Good students have several qualities. For one, they work hard to learn. They ask questions and really try to understand what they read and hear. Also, they take school seriously. They do not wait until the last minute to finish projects. They don't skip homework either. This helps them get good grades. Finally, good students are organized. They stay on top of assignments and due dates.

Students who study and work hard during the year can do better on tests. They are more prepared, so they do not worry. They know the material. Following these steps can help students succeed in the long run.

The passage tells what makes a good student. List three qualities that a good student should have. Then, tell what you would add. What other quality do you think a good student has? Give details and reasons to support your answer.

Answer 1

The pasage said good students work hard to learn. They ask questions and really try to understand. they get good grades. Also students can practice at home. Like writing and reeding. If they do more of that, they will know it better.

What score would you give this answer? Give reasons for your score. When you are finished, discuss the score with your teacher or tutor.

____

____

Answer 2

> A good student works hard to learn, takes school seriusly, and does homework and projects on time. I think staying healthy is good. You shoud get good sleep so you can stay awake in school. And eat the right food. That way your stomach won't growl and distract you.

What score would you give this answer? Give reasons for your score. When you are finished, discuss the score with your teacher or tutor.

____

____

Answer 3

> I wanna be a good student. I will try theese things. My mom say she can halp me study.

What score would you give this answer? Give reasons for your score. When you are finished, discuss the score with your teacher or tutor.

____

____

B. You can practice writing some answers here. When you are done, think about what score they might get. Review them with your teacher or tutor.

DIRECTIONS **Read this passage. Then read the prompt after it. Write your answer on your own paper.**

1.

Your Feet Stink!

Do your feet stink? If they do, what makes them so stinky? Sweat-eating bacteria are what makes your feet stink. The bacteria are attracted to the sweat on your feet. They like to eat it. *Ew*! The bacteria have a strong odor that makes your feet smell bad.

Your feet have over 200,000 sweat glands. Wearing socks and shoes does not help because that traps the sweat to your skin. Bacteria love dark and damp places. The more you sweat, the more your feet will smell.

Some people believe there's only one way to get rid of stinky feet: wash your shoes. Shoes can harbor odors, dirt, and fungus. You can throw most nonleather shoes into a washing machine. A good bath in laundry soap and baking soda gets rid of the smell. What if they still stink? You can sprinkle foot powder into your shoes daily. This keeps away the bacteria.

Here are some ways to prevent stinky feet:

1 **Wash your feet every day.**

2 **Always wear clean socks.**

3 **Try to choose shoes that are made of breathable fabrics.**

4 **Spray a deodorizer in your shoes, or use foot powder. This is especially important for sneakers.**

You learned some things about why feet might smell. Based on what you learned, describe what would make feet smell the worst. What are the ideal conditions for stinky feet? Use information from the passage and your own ideas to support your answer.

Use your own paper to write your answer. When you are finished, score your answer with your teacher or tutor.

2.

DIRECTIONS **Read this poem. Then read the prompt after it. Write your answer on your own paper.**

Rainy Days

Rainy days are sometimes gray,
But birds and squirrels still come out to play.

Mister Sun hides his face in the clouds,
And it's fun to curl up and read aloud.

Sunny days are made for wild outside fun,
But I also like to be calm and quiet
when there is no sun.

What can you tell about the person speaking in this poem? What kind of personality does the narrator have? Describe what you think he or she is like based on this poem. Use information from the poem and your own ideas to support your answer.

Use your own paper to write your answer. When you are finished, score your answer with your teacher or tutor.

Chapter 2
Kinds of Literature

This chapter covers DOK levels 1–3 and the following third grade strands and standards (for full standards, please see Appendix A):

Reading Literature: 1, 2, 4, 10
Reading Foundational Skills: 4
Writing: 1–5, 8, 10
Speaking and Listening: 1.c–d, 2–4
Language: 5 (1–6 in writing tasks)

Literature is like shoes. How is that possible? Well, imagine you are going to the mall. You need to buy a new pair of shoes. A shoe store is one kind of store in the mall. The shoe store has all kinds of shoes. There are boots, sandals, tennis shoes, and so on. They are all shoes, but they are different types of shoes.

Literature has groups just like shoes do. A type of literature is called a genre.

Genres of Literature

What is a **genre**? If you have not seen this word before, it is a good new word to know! Genre (pronounced ***zhon***-rah) means "type or category." There are four main genres (kinds) of literature. They are **fiction**, **nonfiction**, **drama**, and **poetry**. These are big genres (like stores in a mall). They have little genres in them (like the types of things each store sells).

Fiction

Fiction is the term for made-up stories. Fiction stories have characters, places, and events that are all made up by the author. Some fiction stories have real people or places in them. But what happens in the story is invented by the author. On the following page are some kinds of fiction.

Chapter 2

Here are some of the kinds of fiction:

Genre	Description	Examples
Fable	a short story with a lesson in it; fables often have talking animals as characters	Aesop's fables
Fairy Tale	usually starts with "once upon a time" and ends with "happily ever after;" usually has magic in it	"Cinderella" "Goldilocks and the Three Bears"
Legend	a story about the history of a place or people; like a tall tale, it can have real people in it; tells something important about the place or people it is about	the legend of the Fountain of Youth the legend of King Arthur
Mystery	a story with characters who have to solve a puzzle or crime	*Scoop Snoops* by Constance Hiser *Mystery Ranch* by Gertrude Warner
Myth	a story with supernatural characters (people and animals with special powers) that explains something in nature	stories about how the earth was created or how certain animals came to be Greek mythology, like the story of Pandora and her magic box

Genre	Description	Examples
Science Fiction	a story with scientific facts or made-up science of the future; sometimes has aliens or takes place on another planet	*Ned Feldman, Space Pirate* by Daniel Pinkwater *The Time Machine* by H. G. Wells
Tall Tale	a short story with largerthan-life heroes; sometimes based on real people, but the stories are made up and sometimes are very funny	"Paul Bunyan Tames the Whistling River" "The Saga of Pecos Bill"

Fiction also has groups based on how long a written story is.

A **novel** is a long fiction story. All stories have a beginning, middle, and end. Some stories are broken up into chapters. Each chapter builds on the chapter before it.

Examples: *Mr. Popper's Penguins* by Richard and Florence Atwater
Because of Winn-Dixie by Kate DiCamillo

Short stories can be any type of literature, like mystery, adventure, or science fiction. Most are between ten and fifty pages long. Like longer stories, short stories also have a beginning, middle, and end.

Examples: "Jack and the Beanstalk"
"The Red Velvet Ribbon"

Chapter 2

Nonfiction

Nonfiction means "not fiction." Nonfiction is about real people, places, and events. Nothing is made up. It tells about real life. Sometimes it is about the past. Other times, it is about things happening now or people living now. Here are some examples of nonfiction.

Genre	Description	Examples
Article	short writing in a newspaper or magazine about a real event or topic	"Dog Rescues Owner from Fire" in the local newspaper "What to See When You Visit Rome" in a travel magazine
Autobiography	the story of a real person's life written by that person; the word "I" is used because the person is writing about his or her own life	*Anne Frank: The Diary of a Young Girl* by Anne Frank *Africa in My Blood: An Autobiography in Letters* by Jane Goodall
Biography 	the story of a real person's life written by someone else; the word "he" or "she" is used because the author is writing about another person (you will read about point of view in chapter 3)	*Johnny Appleseed* by Jane Kurtz *Joan of Arc* by Diane Stanley
History 	an article or a book about one or more events in the past	*The Reb and the Redcoats* by Constance Savery *The Scottish Chiefs* by Jane Porter

Genre	Description	Examples
Letter	personal writing from one person to another; also letters to the editor in newspapers and magazines, which are letters that readers write and want to get published for other people to read	a letter you write to your grandmother, a letter published in the newspaper that tells the author's opinion about a new shop in town, or even an e-mail message to a friend
Speech	writing down what you want to say out loud; if you will speak in class, jotting down on a note card what you will talk about	the president's State of the Union Address that's shown on TV "The Gettysburg Address" by Abraham Lincoln
Textbooks	books about a topic you are learning, like social studies, science, or art	*History of the United States* *Third Grade Biology* *How to Paint a Portrait*

Drama

Drama includes short and long plays. Drama is written for actors to perform. A play can be read aloud. It also can be acted out on stage. Drama is written in lines of dialogue (talking). It also includes stage directions. These explain what the director and the actors should do.

Drama is not written in chapters. Instead, a play is broken up into scenes. Longer plays might have acts and scenes. These are like chapters in a book. Each scene might have a different setting or change which characters are on stage.

Here is an example from a short play. You can see what each character is supposed to say. You can also see the stage directions in italics (the words written in slanted letters).

> ELLEN: Well, I'm not staying here to find out what happens next.
>
> JAKE: Me neither! For all we know, a ghost will come out of the closet!
> ELLEN: [*rolling her eyes*] Don't be silly. But, we sure don't want to be here if the people who own this spooky old house come back!
>
> [*They head for the door.*]

Poetry

Poetry is a special kind of writing. It does not follow the normal rules of sentences or punctuation. A poem is usually written in lines. Many poems are broken up into sections called stanzas. Poems can make you feel some emotion or think about something. Some tell stories. Others show thoughts or feelings about an idea or object. Some rhyme (have similar sounds at the ends of lines). Others do not.

Here is an example of a poem. This is one that does rhyme. Read it out loud to hear the words that rhyme.

Baa, Baa, Black Sheep
from the rhymes of Mother Goose

1 Baa, baa, black sheep,
2 Have you any wool?
3 Yes, sir, yes, sir,
4 Three bags full.

5 One for my master,
6 One for my dame,
7 And one for the little boy
8 Who lives in the lane.

You can see that lines 2 and 4 have the same end sounds (*wool*, *full*). Lines 6 and 8 almost rhyme (*dame*, *lane*). Lines 1 through 4 are the first stanza. Lines 5 through 8 are the second stanza.

Reading List

The best way to learn more about literature is to read! Here are some books to check out. Ask your teacher or a librarian for more examples of books you might like

Fiction
Cam Jansen and the Mystery of the Monster Movie by David Adler
Emily Eyefinger by Duncan Ball
Freckle Juice by Judy Blume
Muggie Maggie by Beverly Cleary
A Carp in the Bathtub by Barbara Cohen
Dorrie and the Witchville Fair by Patricia Coombs
Chuck and Danielle by Peter Dickinson
Sees Behind Trees by Michael Dorris
Butterfly Boy by Gerardo Suzan
Eating Ice Cream with a Werewolf by Phyllis Green
Jason and the Aliens Down the Street by Gery Greer
Incognito Mosquito, Private Insective by E. A. Hass
The Shrinking of Treehorn by Florence Heide
Millie Cooper, 3B by Charlotte Herman
Big Base Hit by Dean Hughes
Anna, the One and Only by Barbara Joosse
The Case of the Gobbling Squash: A Magic Mystery by Elizabeth Levy
Ali, Child of the Desert by Jonathan London
I'll Meet You at the Cucumbers by Lilian Moore
The Littles Go Exploring by John Peterson

Nonfiction
Anno's Math Games by Mitsumasa Anno
Flight by Robert Burleigh
Ellis Island: Coming to the Land of Liberty by Raymond Bial
Finding Out about Things at Home by Eliot Humberstone
Comeback!: Four True Stories by Jim O'Connor
W. Bugs by Nancy Parker
Sod Houses on the Great Plains by Glen Rounds
Volcanoes by Seymour Simon
Drama
Little Wolf's Book of Badness by Anthony Clark
Multicultural Plays for Children by Pamela Gerke
Pushing up the Sky: Seven Native American Plays for Children by Joseph Bruchac
Poetry
Roses Are Pink, Your Feet Really Stink by Diane DeGroat
The Cat in the Hat by Dr. Seuss
In the Wild by David Elliott
A Book of Nonsense by Edward Lear
Riddle Romp by Guilio Maestro
In Enzo's Splendid Gardens by Patricia Polacco

Practice 1: Genres

RL 1, 2, 10, **RF** 4, **W** 1, 2 **L** 5 (DOK 1–3)

DIRECTIONS **Read each passage, and then answer the questions.**

Worms

There are many kinds of worms. They live in almost all parts of the world. They even live at the bottom of the ocean. Most worms live in the dirt.

Worms are good for dirt. They help air go through the dirt. They eat dead plants. This is good for plants. It helps new plants grow.

Worms have been on earth for a long time. They have been around since the dinosaurs. Worms have been good for dirt and plants for a long time!

1 What type of nonfiction is this passage?

A Speech

B Autobiography

C Article

D Biography

2 How do you know that this passage belongs to that genre?

A It gives you facts.

B It is spoken aloud.

C It tells about a real person.

D It is from someone's diary.

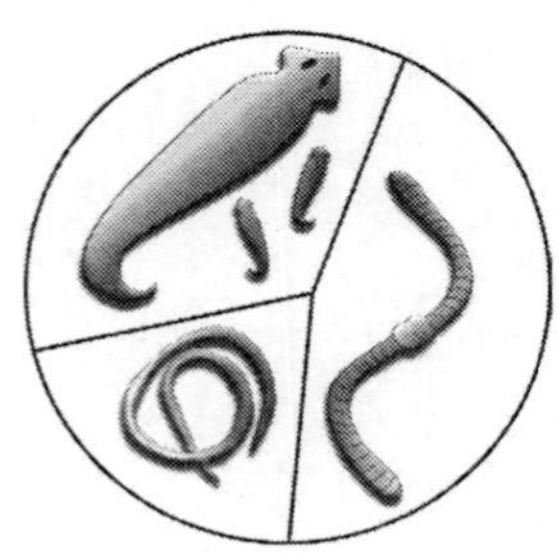

3 Where would you most likely find this passage?

A In a newspaper

B In a science book

C In a book of myths

D In a social studies book

Con Tiqui

There was no light in the world. All the people were sad. They could not see anything. Con Tiqui popped out of a lake. He wanted to help.

He felt bad for people. He put his shiny crown in the sky. It became the sun. People were happy because they were able to see. Con Tiqui told people to explore the world. He showed them how to build things.

Con Tiqui felt better. He went back home to the bottom of the water.

4 How do you know that this is a myth?

A The story teaches the reader a lesson.

B It explains something in nature.

C It uses talking animals to tell the story.

D It is written in lines that rhyme.

5 What shows you that Con Tiqui is not a regular person? Describe what makes Con Tiqui special.

____

____

Celery

by Ogden Nash

Celery, raw,
Develops the jaw,
But celery, stewed,
Is more quietly chewed.

6 What kind of writing is "Celery"?

A A fable

B An article

C A poem

D A speech

7 What happens to celery when it is stewed (cooked)? Based on the passage, what is it like before and after being stewed?

____

____

Chapter 2

Lessons in Literature

Many stories, poems, and plays have a **message** or a **lesson**. A message about life is called a **theme**. A lesson in a story is called a **moral**. Have you ever read a fable? At the end, it might say, "The moral of the story is …"'

DIRECTIONS **Read this story, and then answer the question after it.**

The Cat and the Birds

by Aesop

A Cat heard that the Birds in a certain house were feeling sick. He dressed himself up as a doctor. They would not see he was a cat, and he could eat them. He walked with a cane and had a doctor's bag full of things a doctor carries. He went to call on them. He knocked at the door and asked how they were. The Cat said that if they were ill, he would be happy to help cure them. The Birds replied, "We are all very well. And we will stay well if you go away and leave us as we are."

1 What is the lesson in this passage?

- **A** Never trust a dressed-up cat.
- **B** Birds are much smarter than cats.
- **C** No one wants to go to the doctor.
- **D** Do not let strangers into your house.

What lesson did you see in the story? Most likely it is saying that it's good to be careful. So, answer D would be the best one. Like the Birds, you need to be smart and not let strangers in the door. The Cat's disguise did not fool them!

Practice 2: Lessons in Literature

RL 1, 2, 10, **RF** 4, **W** 1, 2 (DOK 1–3)

DIRECTIONS **Read each passage. Answer the questions that follow.**

The Lamb and the Wolf

by Aesop

A Lamb sat up on the roof of a house. Looking down, he saw a Wolf passing under him. He began to shout to his enemy. "Murderer and thief," he cried. "What are you doing here, near honest folks' houses? How dare you come here, where your evil deeds are known?"

1 What kind of story is this?

A A mystery

B A fable

C Science fiction

D A tall tale

2 Which statement best describes the message of this passage?

A It is easy to be brave from a safe distance.

B Pride is a lamb's best friend.

C Calling someone names is very foolish.

D Speaking to a wolf shows bravery.

George Washington

George Washington grew up on a farm in Virginia. He worked hard on the farm. He got big and strong. His parents taught him to be honest and to always tell the truth.

People tell many stories about George Washington. One famous story is about George when he was a little boy. He had gotten a shiny new hatchet. He wanted to try it out, so he chopped up as much wood as he could find. When there was no more wood, he chopped down his father's prized cherry tree. When his father found out, he asked George what happened. Sad that he had done wrong, George answered honestly, "I cannot tell a lie. I chopped down the cherry tree." George's father was proud of his son for telling the truth. That is how George Washington was known for his honesty.

When he grew up, George helped explore the country. He made maps of places that had no maps yet. He was a soldier too. He fought to protect the settlers in the colonies. He became a great general when America fought to be free from British rule.

George Washington became the first president of the United States. The nation's capital—Washington, DC—is named for him. He was a very good president. Today, George Washington is known as "The Father of Our Country."

3 What genre of writing is this passage?

A Fiction

B Nonfiction

C Drama

D Poetry

4 The second paragraph tells a legend about George Washington. What main message does it tell?

____

____

Writing about Literature

You will read all kinds of books, stories, poems, and articles in class. At times, the teacher will ask you to write about them. You might need to do some different kinds of writing about what you read.

Write to Explain

You might have to write a report about a story or book you read. When you do, you must **explain** what it was about. You will also need to describe the people and places in the story.

Sometimes you will write to answer questions. You might need to write about what problem was solved in a story. Or you might need to tell what the words and images mean in a poem.

Tell Your Opinion

In class, do you talk about whether you liked a story you read? When your teacher asks you if you liked a story, do you just answer "Yes" or "No"? If you do, your teacher probably will ask you to give some details about your **opinion**. You also might be asked a specific question. For example, you might have to write about why a character in a story did something. You need to use facts from the story to support your opinion.

Write a Story

Sometimes in class, you will be asked to **write a story**. When you do, you can tell about events, experiences, and your own ideas. You might also write a poem or a short play. As you write, you can use words in creative ways, as you have learned authors do.

Practice 3: Writing about Literature

RL 2, 10, **RF** 4, **W** 1–3, 8, 10 **L** 1–6 (DOK 3)

DIRECTIONS

Read the passage, and then follow the directions that come after it. Use your own paper to write your essay. Make sure your writing is clear and that your essay has a beginning, middle, and end.

Pandora's Box

In Greek myths, Pandora was the first woman on Earth. She was created to be like Aphrodite, the most beautiful goddess. Gods gave Pandora many gifts and talents. She had lovely clothes, musical ability, and great charm. The highest goddess, Hera, gave her a constant curiosity. Pandora always wanted to know more. Hermes, the messenger god, gave her a mysterious box. He warned her never to open it.

Pandora carried the box with her all the time. But she was curious. One day, she could not take it any longer. She opened the box. From it, she released greed, famine, anger, terror, disease, and death. They escaped and spread over the Earth. She realized what the gods had done. For each gift she had received, a curse had been hidden in the box. Pandora tried to shut the lid, but its contents had already escaped. They could not be put back.

However, one thing had not escaped. Still in the box was one more element—hope. It stayed locked inside. Pandora was afraid to ever go near the box again.

Today, we sometimes say that a person is "opening Pandora's box." This means that what the person is doing may be harmful and hard to change back.

A Write a response on your own paper. In your essay, tell what it means that hope was left inside the box. How does hope help people to overcome the curses that were released from Pandora's box?

B For more practice with writing, write your own myth. Study the table on page 16 that tells you what makes a story a myth. In your myth, tell how something happened. You can make up your own characters and events.

Activity

W 3.a–d, 4, **SL** 1.a–d

In a group, choose a story that one of you wrote. Turn it into a play. Pick who will play each character in the story, and write out the dialogue each person will say. Include stage directions to explain how things should be done by the actors. Then act out the play for another group or for the class.

Chapter 2 Summary

RL 1, 2, 4, 10, **RF** 4, **W** 1–5, 8, 10, **SL** 1.c–d, 2–4, **L** 5 (1–6 in writing tasks)

A **genre** means a type of literature. There are four main genres of literature: fiction, nonfiction, drama, and poetry.

A **fiction** story is made up or created by the author. Examples of fiction are novels, folktales, legends, myths, and short stories.

Nonfiction stories are about real people or real events. Examples of nonfiction are articles, autobiographies, and biographies.

Drama is writing that is meant to be spoken or acted out. Drama includes both short and long plays.

Poetry is verse written to stir thought and feeling in the reader.

Literature can have a **message** or a **lesson**. A message about life is called a **theme**. A lesson in a story is called a **moral**.

Sometimes you will **write about literature**. You might need to **explain**, give your **opinion**, or **write a story**.

For more practice with this chapter's material, see the Literature Review on page 51.

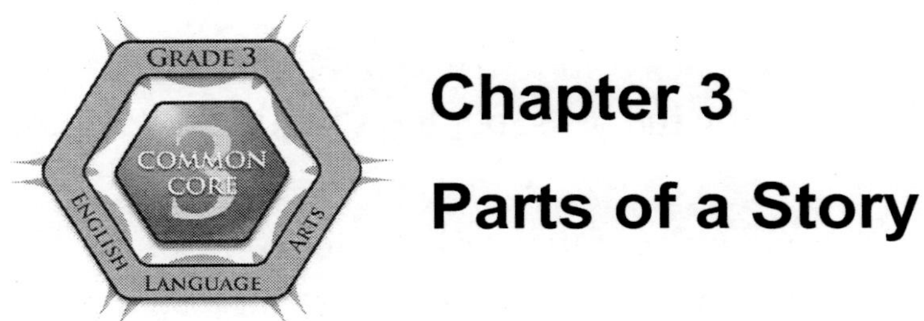

Chapter 3
Parts of a Story

This chapter covers DOK levels 1–3 and the following third grade strands and standards (for full standards, please see Appendix A):

Reading Literature: 1, 2, 3, 5–7, 9–10
Reading Foundational Skills: 4
Writing: 1–5, 7, 10
Speaking and Listening: 1.c–d, 2–4
Language: (1–6 in writing tasks)

There are many parts to a story. If a story didn't have these parts, it would be boring. In this chapter, we will talk about the parts of a story.

Characters

A **character** is someone in a story. It can be a person. It can be an animal. It can even be an object that in real life would not be alive.

Examples of Characters	
Type	**Examples**
person	Harry Potter, Ramona, Batman
animal	Nemo, Bolt, Bugs Bunny
object	SpongeBob SquarePants, Transformers

Characters do things. They make the story happen. They all have **traits**. Some characters are tall, and some are short. Some are funny. Others are mean. Try to think of characters as real people.

Think about the **feelings** of characters in stories. Just like real people, they can be happy, sad, excited, or bored. They also have **motivations**. These are the reasons for their actions. For example, Winnie the Pooh takes a risk when he tries to get honey from a beehive. He does this because he loves honey so much.

In other words, his love for honey motivates him to try to get honey from the beehive. He knows he might get stung by the bees, but he is willing to take the chance!

The **actions** of a character tell you much about him or her. Notice how the character talks to others, treats others, and makes decisions. What a character does also adds to the events of the story. Look at this short scene from a play.

ERIN: Marcy, have you seen my favorite pen?

MARCY: You mean the one that plays "Take Me Out to the Ball Game" when you click it?

ERIN: Yep, that's the one. Have you seen it?

MARCY: [*in a teasing tone*] Well, it depends.

ERIN: [*confused*] Depends on what? What in the world are you talking about?

MARCY: Have you seen my slice of chocolate cake?

[*The girls burst into giggles.*]

What can you tell about Erin and Marcy? Well, you can see that they know each other very well. Marcy knows all about Erin's favorite pen. She then jokingly accuses Erin of taking her cake. But the girls do not get angry with each other. They laugh about it. This action shows they are good friends.

There are many other ways you can get to know characters. You can **contrast** two of them. That means you can say how they are different from one another. You can also compare them to each other. To **compare** is to see how they are the same. Here is a Venn diagram to show an example:

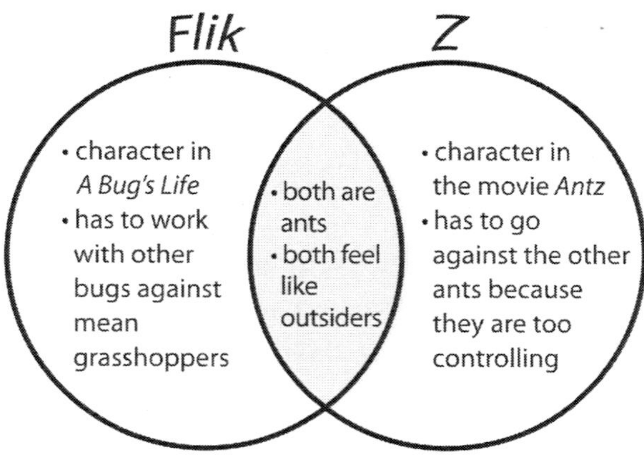

These characters are not from the same place. Their families are not the same. They do not look the same. Seeing how different they are means we can contrast them. But what is the same about them? Well, they are both ants, and both are misfits. That is how we can compare them.

Narrator and Point of View

Every story is told by a **narrator**. This is the person telling the story. Sometimes, a character in the story tells it. Other times, the narrator is not in the story. It is like a storyteller who tells you what the characters do, what they say, and where they go.

Who tells the story is called **point of view**. A character telling a story has his or her own point of view. You can see a good example of how this works in the book *I Was a Third Grade Spy* by Mary Jane Auch. The narrator of the first chapter is Artful the dog. Yes, he is a dog who can talk! Some chapters are told by Artful's owner, Brian. Other chapters are narrated by Brian's friend, Josh. Each character tells the story from his own point of view.

You have your own point of view too. When you read a story, you might even argue with something a character thinks or says. Say you read a story about a boy named Mike. Other kids are mean to Mike, but he wants to be friends with them. This is his motivation. So he pretends they have good reasons for treating him badly. That is Mike's point of view. But you see that he should stand up for himself. That is your point of view.

Setting

The **setting** is the place and time of a story. An author can write about any time or place. The story can take place in the past, as far back as the time of the dinosaurs. It can happen in the present day and in a place you know well. It even can be set in the future in outer space!

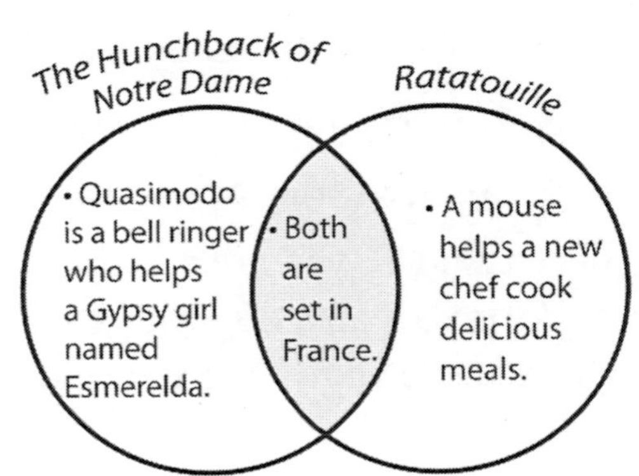
The Hunchback of Notre Dame
Ratatouille
• Quasimodo is a bell ringer who helps a Gypsy girl named Esmerelda.
• Both are set in France.
• A mouse helps a new chef cook delicious meals.

Some stories are set in the same place. Often this makes it easy for you to compare them. Here is another Venn diagram as an example:

Both stories are set in France. This is how we can compare them. But the stories are very different. One has a rat as a main character and is about making wild dreams come true. The other story is about accepting people no matter how they look—what is inside a person is most important. This is how we can contrast the two stories.

Pictures in Stories

Many stories include pictures. Pictures in a book are called **illustrations**. llustrations often help to set the mood of a story. They help you understand more about the setting and characters. They allow you to see what you are reading. Look at this example.

Playing in the Sand

"This will be the biggest sandcastle ever!" Jose said. He used a blue bucket to add more sand to the tower of the castle. "Let's put a river around it," Andy said. He started digging a trench. Jose laughed and helped him dig all around the base of the castle. They poured in water from a bucket. The moat now protected their mighty sandcastle.

How does the illustration help you understand the story?

A It shows where the boys are playing.

B It shows what good friends the boys are.

C It shows the size and shape of the castle.

D It shows how bright and sunny the day is.

If you said C, you are correct. The picture does not show the boys. So, it can't be A or B. It also does not show the sunshine, so it can't be D. Answer C is best. The picture shows the size and shape of the castle that the boys built.

Practice 1: Characters, Point of View, and Setting

RL 1, 2, 3, 5, 6, 10, **RF** 4 (DOK 1–3)

DIRECTIONS **Read the passage below. Then choose the answer that best describes the character.**

The Ferris Wheel

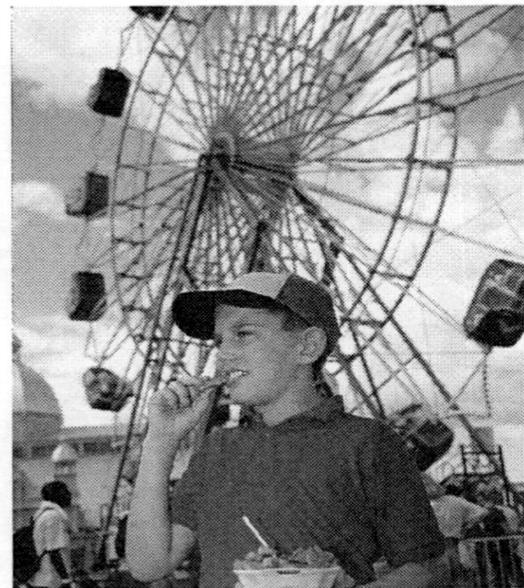

Misha stood in the long line with his friends, Tim and Shane. Tim ate his cotton candy while they waited. Shane had some french fries with a tasty dipping sauce. Misha could not think about eating anything.

This would be the second ride they rode. The first was the bumper cars. Misha loved the bumper cars. He wanted to ride them again. But his friends wanted to ride the ferris wheel. They were laughing and pointing up at the huge turning wheel.

Misha's tummy felt a little sick. He looked up at how high the ferris wheel went. He did not like heights. But he didn't want his friends to know. They would think he was a chicken. So, he waited in line and tried to think about something else. He was glad the line was long.

1 Where are Misha and his friends?

A A school

B The bus stop

C A carnival

D Misha's house

2 What is the main difference between Misha and his friends?

____

____

____

3 Who does the picture show?

A Misha

B Tim

C Shane

D Someone else

4 What does Misha think his friends will do if they know he is scared?

A He thinks they will make fun of him.

B He thinks they will feel sorry for him.

C He thinks they will tell his mother.

D He thinks they will run away from him.

The Emperor's New Clothes

Adapted from the story by Hans Christian Andersen

Many years ago, there was an Emperor. He loved new clothes. He spent all his money on them. He had a different suit for each hour of the day.

One day, two thieves came to the city. They were disguised as tailors. They told people that they could make beautiful clothes of the finest material. The colors were bright. The patterns were amazing. But, they said, these clothes were invisible to anyone who was not worthy. If a person were unfit for the office he held, or was dull or stupid in any way, he would not be able to see the clothes.

"These must indeed be splendid clothes!" thought the Emperor. "If I have such a suit, I can find out who in my realm is unfit for his office. I would also be able to tell the wise from the foolish! I must have these clothes right away." He paid the two men so they could begin work.

The two pretend tailors pretended to work very hard. In reality, they did nothing at all. They asked for the most delicate silk. They wanted the purest gold thread. But they really put both into their own knapsacks. They did their pretend work until late at night.

The Emperor wanted to know how the work was coming. He thought about who to send. After all, someone dull or unfit for his job would not be able to see the fine cloth!

"I will send my faithful old minister," said the Emperor at last. "He will see how the cloth looks; for he is a man of sense, and no one can be more suitable for his office than he is."

So the faithful old minister went to the room where the pretend tailors were pretend working. He saw them working on nothing.

"What is the meaning of this?" he thought. "I cannot see the least bit of cloth." However, he did not say this aloud. "I will never confess that I cannot see the stuff," he thought. So he told the thieves their work was excellent and that he would describe it to the Emperor.

The minister told the Emperor about the fine clothes. In the next few days, the Emperor sent more officers of his court to look at the work. They all came back with glowing reports. None of them wanted to be fired or called stupid!

Finally, the day came! The Emperor would wear the new clothes in a great parade through the city. The pretend tailors stayed up the whole night pretending to finish the clothes. As the sun came up, they shouted, "The Emperor's new clothes are ready!"

Now the Emperor, with all his court, came to the tailors. They raised their arms, as if holding something up. They said, "Here are your Majesty's trousers! Here is the scarf! Here is the shirt! The whole suit is as light as a cobweb. One might think one has nothing at all on—such is the great quality of this delicate cloth."

They pretended to dress the Emperor. They praised how wonderful he looked. All the lords and ladies of the court pretended too.

Now the Emperor walked in the parade. All the people cried out, "Oh! How beautiful! Look at our Emperor's new clothes! How graceful and lovely the fabric is!" In short, no one wanted to allow that he could not see the clothes.

"But the Emperor has nothing at all on!" said a little child.

"Listen to the voice of innocence!" said his father. What the boy had said was whispered all around.

"But he has nothing at all on!" cried out all the people at last.

The Emperor was upset. He knew that the people were right.

5 Who is telling this story?

A The Emperor

B The little boy

C The boy's father

D An unknown narrator

6 What is most likely true about the Emperor?

A He eats so much his clothes don't fit.

B He loves clothes more than anything.

C He gives many gifts to all his people.

D He likes and trusts everyone in his court.

7 What does the author show you about all the people in the court and the city?

A Their most important value is to always tell the truth.

B The people love the Emperor and don't want to upset him.

C They care most about what other people think of them.

D No one has seen such beautiful clothes, so they are excited.

8 What is the setting of this story? What clues in the story tell you this?

____

____

____

Plot

What happens in a story or book is called the **plot**. The plot is the chain of events in the story. Every story has a beginning, middle, and end. Certain things happen at different times. Here are the parts of the plot.

Introduction – how the story starts. In this part, the author usually tells where the story takes place and who the characters are.

Example: Once upon a time, there was a beautiful princess. Her name was Trudy. She lived in a big castle with her father and mother, the king and the queen.

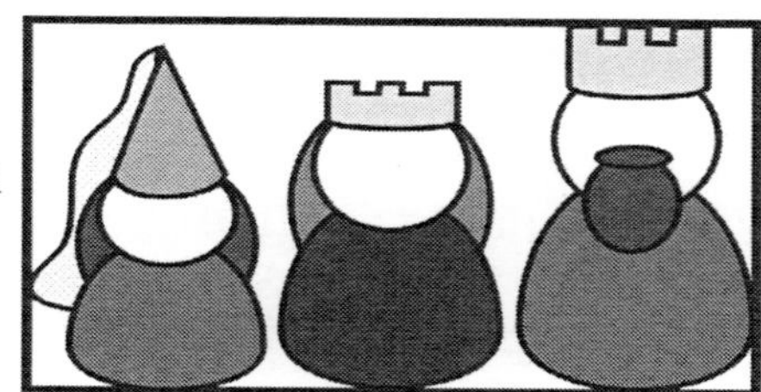

Conflict – the problem the characters face, or a journey that they must take.

Example: One day, Princess Trudy was in her lovely garden. Suddenly, she saw a wild wolf near the cherry tree! It saw her too and let out a low growl. She was afraid. Should she run away?

Rising Action – now, the action in the story gets exciting.

Example: Trudy looked around and saw a sharp garden axe not far from where she stood. Maybe she could use it to defend herself! She turned and ran. She heard the wolf growl and run after her.

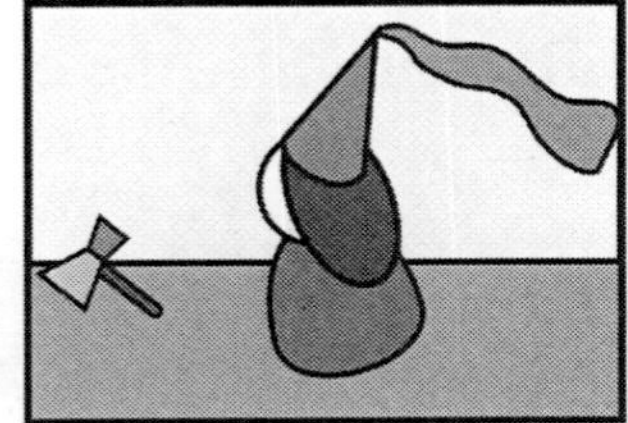

Climax – the turning point in a story. The action of the story is at its highest, most suspenseful point.

Example: Then the wolf spoke pounced! He knocked Trudy to the ground, inches from the axe. "Princess, the ogre in the woods put a curse on me. I need a gift from you, so he will remove the curse." Trudy's mind was racing—should she reach for the axe? Or should she believe the wolf? Her true nature was to be kind and gentle, so she gave the wolf an emerald ring from her finger. The wolf took it in his teeth and ran off.

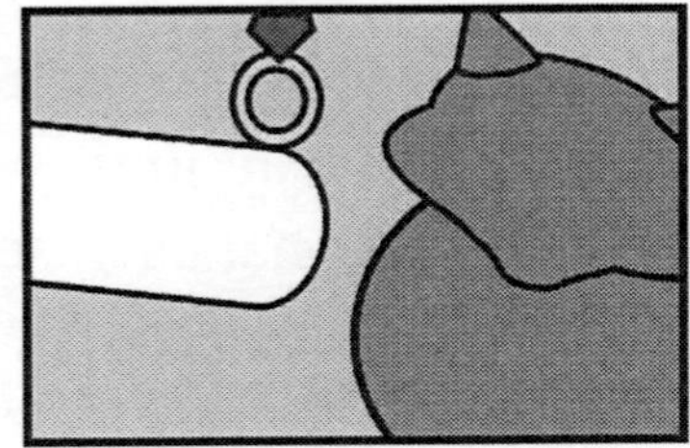

Chapter 3

Falling Action – the action in the story slows down. The main character's life may begin to return to normal. It may even be better.

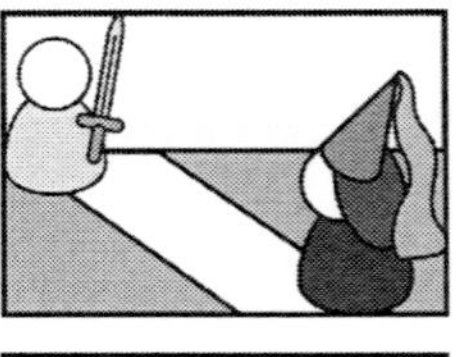

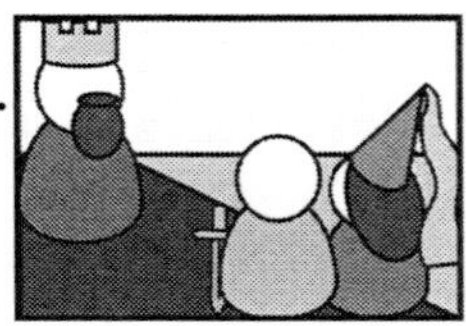

Example: A week later, a brave and handsome knight came to the castle. His name was Malcolm. He was from a nearby kingdom. Trudy felt like she knew him, but she didn't know why. Malcolm asked the king if he could marry Princess Trudy. The king agreed. So Trudy and Malcolm were engaged.

Resolution – the ending of a story. All conflict is settled.

Example: Example: One day in the garden, Malcolm said, "I want to thank you." Trudy did not understand. He told her that he had been the terrible wolf! He had been under a spell. He was afraid Trudy might kill him or call the guards. But instead she had given him the gift he needed so the ogre would lift the curse. "Thank you for being so gentle and trusting," Malcolm told Trudy. "I shall spend the rest of my life rewarding you for your kindness."

You can see how **parts of the story build on what happened before**. The end is not fun to read until you know how the story started. In the story about Princess Trudy, say that each section you read about is one chapter. What if you left out chapter 3, the climax? The story would not make sense anymore. Authors work hard to make the parts of a story fit. Now, look at this question about the story.

Why does Trudy feel like she knows Malcolm?

A She has heard about knights from nearby kingdoms.

B She once had a dream about him a long time ago.

C She met him when he had been turned into a wolf.

D She was introduced to him by her father.

Did you pick answer C? You are correct! You know from reading the whole story that Trudy and Malcolm already met—even though he had the shape of a wolf then. But he even talked to her. So, she remembers something about him. This shows how parts of the plot build on what happened earlier.

THEME

As you read in chapter 2, the **theme** is the message in a piece of literature. It tells the reader something about life. Themes talk about experiences that people everywhere share. For example, people all over the world know what love is. One theme could be "love is blind." Here are some other examples of themes.

- Don't be greedy.
- Honesty is a good trait to have.
- There are things worth fighting for.

Most times, a writer does not come right out and tell you the theme. You need to find the theme by looking for clues. To find the theme, it helps to do the following:

- Look for hints in the title.
- Think about how the story is told.
- Write one sentence about what the message seems to be.

PLOT AND THEME IN A SERIES

Some authors write series of books with the same or similar characters. Examples include the books *The Mouse and the Motorcycle* and *Ralph S. Mouse*, both written by Beverly Cleary.

You can **compare and contrast** the themes, setting, and plots as you read each book in that series. Another example is the Harry Potter series by J. K. Rowling. All the books in this series have the same set of friends—Harry, Ron, and Hermione. But they go through a new adventure in each book.

Practice 2: Plot and Theme

RL 1, 2, 3, 5, 7, 10, **RF** 4 (DOK 1–2)

DIRECTIONS **Read the passages. Answer the questions after each one.**

The Shepherd Boy

from a fable by Aesop

There was once a young shepherd boy. He tended his sheep at the foot of a mountain near a dark forest. It was kind of lonely for him all day. So he thought up a plan by which he could get a little company and have some fun.

He ran down toward the village, calling out, "Wolf, wolf!" The villagers came running out to help, and some of them stopped to talk with him for a long time. This pleased the boy so much that a few days later, he tried the same trick. And again the villagers came running to help him.

But a few days after this, a wolf actually did come out from the forest. The sheep began to bleat in fear. The boy again cried out, "Wolf, wolf!"

Nothing happened. He shouted louder: "Wolf, wolf!" But this time, no villagers came out. The boy had fooled them twice before, so they thought he was doing it again. Nobody came to help him. So the wolf made a good meal of the boy's flock.

1 When the people find out the shepherd boy has lied to them, what happens?

A The wolf gets really hungry and finally eats the boy.

B The villagers don't believe what he says anymore.

C The sheep all run away and have to be rounded up.

D The villagers decide to believe what the boy says.

2 What can a reader learn from seeing what happens to the shepherd boy?

A If you lie, no one will believe you when you tell the truth.

B When you are in danger, be sure to tell people what's wrong.

C Being lonely can make people act in strange and mean ways.

D A wolf can scare anyone enough to lie when they need to.

3 What is the resolution of this story?

A When the boy decides to yell "Wolf!" to get some company

B When the villagers figure out the boy is lying to them

C When the boy realizes a wolf really is attacking his sheep

D When the villagers stay away and the wolf eats the flock

4 How does this picture help you understand the story?

A It reveals how very scary the wolf was.

B It shows the kind of sheep the boy had.

C It explains how hard the boy's job was.

D It shows how angry the villagers were.

5 Read these events from the story. Put them in order. Write 1 next to what happened first, 2 next to what happened next, and 3 next to what happened last.

_____ The shepherd boy yelled "Wolf!" but no one came.

_____ The shepherd boy yelled "Wolf!" and the villagers ran to help him.

_____ A real wolf came and scared the sheep.

DIRECTIONS

Now you will read a passage. "The Crow and the Pitcher" is adapted from a fable by Aesop. You will read a few lines of it at a time. Then you will decide which part of the story it is. Write the letter of the story part in the blank after each question.

A Resolution

B Rising action

C Introduction

D Climax

E Conflict

F Falling action

> There was a crow in the forest. He had been wandering for days. He could not find water. The creek had dried up, and he was very thirsty.

6 What part of the plot is this section? ________

> Then he came upon a pitcher. Someone had left it outside, and it had caught some rainwater. But when the crow put his beak into the mouth of the pitcher, he could not reach the bottom where the water was.

7 What part of the plot is this section? ________

> He tried, and he tried. He knew that if he did not get water, he would die of thirst. Maybe he could tip the pitcher … but no, that would spill the water. Maybe he could peck through the side of the pitcher … No, the pitcher was too hard. What could he do?

8 Which part of the plot is this section? ________

As he was about to give up, he had a brilliant thought. Maybe there is another way to get at the water! He picked up a pebble and dropped it into the water. Then he picked up more pebbles and dropped them in one by one. As they settled on the bottom of the pitcher, the water rose toward the mouth of the pitcher!

9 What part of the plot is this section? ________

Finally, the water was up high enough that the crow could reach it. He drank and drank. His thirst was gone. His bright idea had saved his life.

10 What part of the plot is this section? ________

The crow learned a valuable lesson that day. Many times, a problem can be solved little by little if you take the time to think about the best solution.

11 Which part of the plot is this section? ________

12 Now think of all the parts of the fable put together. What is the theme of this story?

A Building something with rocks is smart.

B All animals need water to survive.

C Working through a problem pays off.

D Crows are very intelligent birds.

Practice 3: Writing about Literature

RL 1, 2, 3, 5, 6, 10, **RF** 4, **W** 2, 3, **L** 1–6 (DOK 3)

Think about the two stories you just read in Practice 2—the one about the shepherd boy and the other about the crow. The two characters handled their problems in very different ways.

A. Write about what one character could learn from the other. Which one? What could he learn from the way the other character acted? Tell how the other character could teach him a new way to solve a problem. Use your own paper to write your essay. Make sure your writing is clear and has a beginning, middle, and end.

B. Now, write a story about a time when you figured out how to get what you needed. What approach did you take? Was it easy? Or did it take a long time to work out? Use your own paper to write your essay. Be sure your story has enough detail, and make it interesting to read.

Activity

W 3.a–d, **SL** 1.a–d, 2, 4

In a group, pick a story that you all know well. It could be a fairy tale you all have heard, or it might be a story you read in school. Now change one major thing about it. For example, say the setting is outer space. Or, instead of being a person, say the main character is a duck. Talk about how the story would be different. Write down the main points that would change. Then present the changed story to the rest of the class.

Chapter 3 Summary

RL 1, 2, 3, 5–7, 9–10, **RF** 4, **W** 1–5, 7, 10, **SL**1.c–d, 2–4, **L** (1–6 in writing tasks)

A **character** is a person, animal, or object that does **actions** in a story. Each one has **traits**, **motivations**, and **feelings**. That's how you get to know them.

Setting is the time and the place a story happens.

Many stories include **illustrations** that help you understand more about the setting and characters.

Plot is what happens in a story. The plot has several parts. They include **introduction**, **conflict**, **rising action**, **climax**, **falling action**, and **resolution**. All the **parts build on what happened earlier**.

Theme is the message in a piece of literature.

When you read a series of stories with the same or similar characters, you can **compare and contrast** the plots, themes, and settings of each story in the series.

For more practice with this chapter's material, see the Literature Review on page 51.

Literature Review

This chapter covers DOK levels 1–3 and the following third grade strands and standards (for full standards, please see Appendix A):

Reading Literature: 1–7, 9–10
Reading Foundational Skills: 4
Writing: 1–5, 7, 8, 10
Speaking and Listening: 4
Language: 1–6

This review will give you more practice with the skills you read about in chapters 2 and 3.

DIRECTIONS **First, read the passages. Answer the questions that follow. Then you will write about what you read.**

Why the Sea Is Salty

One winter long ago, there were two brothers named Ted and Tony. Ted was rich, and Tony was poor. The rich brother lived in a great house, but he was stingy. The poor brother lived in a tiny shack and had no food. "We cannot starve," said Tony to his wife. "I will ask my brother to help us."

Ted was annoyed. He said angrily, "Here, take this meat and go to the dwarfs. They will boil it for you." Tony took the meat and left in search of the dwarfs. He trudged through the snow until he saw the home of the dwarfs.

The Chief Dwarf spotted Tony. "Ho, ho! Who enters our cave?" The dwarfs teased Tony and picked at the meat. They wanted it for their supper.

"What will you give me for the meat?" asked Tony.

"We have no gold," said the dwarfs. "But we can give you this mill."

"Why do I want a mill?" cried Tony. "I am hungry and have come to cook this meat for me and my wife."

"It is a wonderful mill," the Chief Dwarf replied. "It will grind anything in the world, except snow and meat. I will show you how to use it." Tony agreed. He gave them the meat and took the mill. The Chief Dwarf said, "When you wish the mill to grind, use these words:

'Grind, quickly grind, little mill,

Grind, with a right good will!'

"When you wish the mill to stop grinding, you must say, 'Halt, halt, little mill!' The mill will obey you," stated the Chief Dwarf.

Taking the little mill under his arm, the poor brother climbed up the hill, through the snow, until he reached his shack. When he arrived, he put the little mill down on the snow, and said at once,

"Grind, quickly grind, little mill, Grind a HOUSE, with a right good will!"

The little mill ground and ground until there stood, in place of the shack, the finest house in the world. It had large windows, and every room was filled with furniture. By spring, the mill had ground out the last thing that was needed for the house, and the poor brother cried, "Halt, halt, little mill!"

The mill obeyed him. Soon, Tony had everything that he wanted.

The following year, a merchant sailed from a distant land and anchored his ship in the harbor. He visited Tony's home and asked about the mill. He had heard how wonderful it was. "Will it grind salt?" the merchant asked.

"Yes, indeed!" said Tony. "It will grind anything in the whole world, except snow and meat."

"Let me borrow the mill for a short time," said the merchant. He thought it would be easier to fill his ship with salt from the mill than to make a long voyage to buy salt for the people of his land. Tony agreed, and the merchant went away with the mill. He did not wait to find out how to stop the grinding. He went back aboard the ship, and he cried out,

"Grind, quickly grind, little mill, Grind SALT, with a right good will!"

The mill ground salt, and more salt, and still more salt. When the ship was full of salt, the merchant cried, "Now you must stop, little mill." The little mill did not stop. It kept on grinding salt.

The captain shouted, "We shall be lost! The ship will sink!"

One of the sailors called, "Throw the mill overboard!" So, overboard went the wonderful mill, down to the bottom of the deep sea. The captain and his crew sailed home with the cargo of salt, and the mill kept on grinding salt at the bottom of the sea.

And that is why the sea is salty. (At least, that's what some people say.)

Practice 1: "Why the Sea Is Salty"

RL 1–6, 9–10, **RF** 4, **SL** 4, **L**1–6

DIRECTIONS **Answer these questions about the passage you just read.**

1 DOK 1

What did the rich brother give to the poor brother?

A Salt
B Gold
C Meat
D Porridge

2 DOK 1

Why do the dwarfs want to trade the mill?

A It can't grind snow, and they want it to snow.
B It can't grind meat, and they want the meat.
C They are tired of asking the mill for everything.
D They want poor Tony to have what he needs.

Literature Review

3

DOK 3

What time of year is it when the story starts? Tell how you know what season it is.

____

____

____

4

DOK 2

Look at how the author describes Ted in the first paragraph. Based on this, what does stingy mean?

A Happy
B Selfish
C Skinny
D Generous

5

DOK 2

What lets you know that this passage is a made-up story?

A The dwarfs give instructions to Tony.
B The little mill is able to listen to people.
C The rich brother is mean to the poor brother.
D The merchant doesn't return the mill to Tony.

6

DOK 1

Why did the mill keep grinding when the merchant told it to stop?

A The merchant didn't use the right words.
B Tony broke the mill by using it too much
C The mill did not like the merchant's voice.
D The dwarfs put a curse on the little mill.

7

DOK 2

What lesson might readers learn from reading this passage?

A It is important to listen to instructions.
B You will like the ocean if you like salt.
C Being kind to others has many rewards.
D Poor people are nicer than rich people.

8

DOK 3

How do you think the merchant feels at the end of the story? Is that how you would feel if you were the merchant?

____

____

____

How Salty Is the Ocean?

You might know that our planet has many seas and oceans. About 70 percent of the earth is covered by salt water. Unlike most lakes and rivers, the water in the ocean tastes salty. In fact, it has so much salt in it that you can't drink it. How did it get that way?

Almost every culture has folk stories and myths about how the oceans became salty. In truth, the answer is as simple as falling off a log. Salt in the sea comes from rocks on land.

Salt is a mineral. It is a kind of rock. As the rain falls, it very slowly dissolves bits of rock. This is called erosion. The tiny bits of rock dissolve in the water and are washed away. They are carried all the way to the ocean.

In addition, salt also comes up from under the sea. There are volcanoes at the bottom of the sea. As hot air rises from them, it heats the water too. In the hot water many minerals get dissolved. These come from the sea floor.

Why Is It Easier to Float in Salt Water?

All water has some dissolved minerals in it. But salt water has more than fresh water. That makes it thicker. In science, this is called *density.* Salt water has more density than fresh water. The denser the water, the more weight it can hold up.

Literature Review

You can do an experiment.

1 Get ten large plastic cups and a carton of eggs. (Before you grab the eggs, ask if you can use them!)

2 With a marker, write the numbers 0 to 10 on the outside of the cups. Line them up in order.

3 Fill the cups with fresh water. Now, try floating an egg on the first cup (the one that has 0 on it, for zero salt). It sinks, right? That's because the density of the egg is greater than the density of the water.

4 Next, put a tablespoon of salt in the second cup with the 1 on it. Mix it well so it dissolves in the water. Try floating the egg again. It still sinks.

5 Keep putting salt in the cups. Put two tablespoons in the cup marked 2, three in the cup marked 3, and so on. Test an egg in each one until the egg floats.

How much salt needed to be in the cup of water before the egg floated?

Practice 2: "How Salty Is the Ocean?"

RL 1–7, 9–10, **RF** 4, **SL** 4, **L** 1–6

DIRECTIONS **Answer these questions about the passage you just read.**

1

DOK 3

Read this sentence from the second paragraph.

In truth, the answer is as simple as falling off a log.

What does "simple as falling off a log" mean?

____

____

____

2

DOK 1

What type of nonfiction is this passage?

A Biography
B History
C Article
D Letter

3

DOK 2

How do you know that this passage belongs to that genre?

A It tells about a person's life.
B It has scientific facts in it.
C It is meant to be acted out.
D It has a plot and a setting.

4

DOK 3

Look at the illustration. How does it help you understand the experiment?

____

____

____

Practice 3: Write about the Passages

W 1–5, 7, 8, 10, **L** 1–6 (DOK 3)

DIRECTIONS **On your own paper, write about these two passages.**

A. Compare and Contrast the Passages

How are they alike? How are they different? How might you use each one for class assignments?

Use your own paper to write your essay. Make sure your writing is clear and has a beginning, middle, and end. Be sure to use support from the passages in your writing.

B. Write a Story

Have you been to the ocean? Have you read stories about the sea, like the one in this chapter? Maybe you have seen shows on TV about ocean life. Write a story that has the ocean in it. It can be a true story about a time you were at the seashore. Or it can be a story you make up, maybe about the life of an animal that lives in the water.

Use your own paper to write your story. Make sure your writing is clear and has a beginning, middle, and end. Be creative!

Activity

W 3.a–d, 4; **SL**1.a–d, 2, 3

Turn your story into a play. Write out dialogue (what each person says) for the characters in it. Give stage directions for the events that happen. Create some simple scenery and props. Then get a group together to be the actors. Act out the play for other groups. Each group can put on a short play. Talk about each play after you watch it.

Practice 4: Research Project

W 1–5, 7, 8, 10, **RF** 4, **SL** 4, **L** 1–6 (DOK 3)

DIRECTIONS

Do some research about a topic related to the passages you read. You can use books and the Internet for your research. Your topic could be something about myths. Or, it might be about salt. It could also be anything about the oceans. Here are a few ideas, or you can come up with your own:

Possible Research Topics

- Myths or fairy tales about salt from another culture
- How to set up a saltwater fish tank
- The difference between saltwater and freshwater fish
- Why people can't drink salt water
- How salt dissolves in water
- Why some lakes have salt water (or, pick just one lake)
- How salt is used to preserve food
- Why people need salt in their diet

Choose your topic. Then do some research. Ask your teacher or the media specialist about the best places to look. Take notes about what you find. Finally, write a report about your topic. Make sure it gives facts in a logical order. Give it a beginning, middle, and end. Add details so people will understand your ideas. As a last step, make sure there are no mistakes in it.

You can also use your paper to give a speech. Ask your teacher to choose a day when everyone can present. Each student can talk about what he or she chose to research. Then, the audience can ask questions.

Chapter 4
Informational Texts

This chapter covers DOK levels 1–3 and the following third grade strands and standards (for full standards, please see Appendix A):

Reading Informational Texts: 1, 2, 4, 6, 9, 10
Reading Foundational Skills: 4
Writing: 2, 4–8, 10
Speaking and Listening: 1–3
Language: 1, 2, 3.a (1–6 in writing tasks)

Informational Text

You read in chapter 1 about nonfiction. *Nonfiction* means "not fiction." It is about real people, places, and events. Nothing is made up. This type of text is called **informational text**. It gives you facts. It might tell about events that really happened. It can inform you about history or science. Or it might tell you about people living today or in the past. Some informational text gives you directions, like a computer manual or a recipe.

What dreams may come
Travelling exhibit showcases the nighttime fantasies of 30 artists

Chapter 4

AUTHOR'S PURPOSE

Authors write for many reasons. The reason why a person writes any text is called the **author's purpose**. Here are some common purposes for writing.

Purposes for Writing

Purpose	Examples
to inform	Newspaper and magazine articles give facts that help you know about what's going on.
to teach	Textbooks you use in school are written to teach you about math or science or reading.
to entertain	Comic books, short stories, and novels like *Junie B. Jones* are all written to entertain. They are fun to read.
to persuade	Some writing wants to convince you about something. It might want you to take some action. For example, a colorful ad might show kids having fun with a toy and say "You can have fun too!" The company that wrote the ad wants you to buy that new toy.
to share a viewpoint	An example of this would be an editorial in a newspaper. In this kind of writing, an author tells how he or she feels. The author usually wants people to agree.

THE AUTHOR AND YOU

Every author is a person just like you. Authors have opinions. At times, what the author feels or thinks will show in the writing. You may agree with the author's point of view, or you may not. When you read, think about **your own point of view**. Consider if your point of view is the same as the author's or not.

Here is an example of a text. You might read this or hear it as a speech. Read the passage. Then tell why the author wrote it and how you feel about the topic.

Charlie for President

Vote for me on November 16! I'll make sure we have hot dogs for lunch! I'll make sure we get an extra hour of recess every Friday! And no homework over holidays! I'll make school fun again! If you want more fun, vote for me. I'm Charlie, and I need your vote!

What is the author's reason for writing this passage?

A To inform readers when they can vote

B To persuade readers to vote for him

C To teach readers about the voting process

D To entertain with stories about school

Did you pick answer B? That's right. Charlie wants you to vote for him. He wrote this speech to convince you to do that.

What is the author's point of view? How is your point of view the same or different?

____

____

____

What did you write? First, your answer should tell about Charlie's point of view. After that, it should tell about your point of view and if it agrees or not with Charlie's.

How does Charlie feel about what he is saying? He seems excited, doesn't he? He wants to make some changes so school will be more fun. He believes other students want this. If they do, they will vote for him.

How do you feel? You might agree that hot dogs, more recess, and no homework on holidays are good changes. If your point of view is the same as Charlie's, he will probably convince you to vote for him! But what if you like pizza better than hotdogs, think recess is boring, or enjoy doing homework during the holidays? You might not be convinced by what Charlie is saying.

Practice 1: Author's Purpose

RI 1 (DOK 2–3)

DIRECTIONS **Read the passages. Then choose the author's purpose for writing each one.**

The Rainy Day Fort

Sometimes it is not possible to build a fort outdoors. Maybe you live in an apartment in a busy city. Or maybe it's too hot or too cold outside. An indoor fort is easy to build. It is also just as much fun as an outdoor fort. All you need are some big pillows and a few blankets. Make walls out of the big pillows and some chairs with high backs. Just arrange them in a square shape. Leave a place to crawl in and out. Next, drape the blankets on the top. Now you can hop inside your cozy fort and have fun!

1 What is the author's purpose for writing this passage?

A To teach readers how to build a fort indoors

B To teach readers how to build a fort outdoors

C To persuade readers not to build forts indoors

D To inform readers how forts can be dangerous

The Girl and the Cat

Once upon a time there lived a poor little girl. She was so poor that she had no shoes or jacket to keep her warm in the winter. She would huddle into a ball and wrap herself in the only blanket she owned, which was full of holes.

One night, she heard a strange sound. It was the sound of a cat crying. The little girl went out and found the cat. The cat was thin and cold. The little girl felt sorry for it and brought it back to her house. She shared what little food she had with the cat and wrapped her blanket around it. She petted the cat and talked gently to it.

To her great surprise, the cat talked back! The cat said, "I am the queen of all cats. Every year I test a person's kindness. You have passed the test, and I will reward you." The cat licked its paw, and a necklace appeared. It was a beautiful necklace made of five large white and blue stones. The cat gave it to the little girl. "This necklace is magic. All you have to do is rub each stone three times and make a wish. Whatever you wish for will magically appear."

2 What is the author's purpose for writing this passage?

A To teach readers how to care for cats

B To persuade readers that cats are good luck

C To inform readers about the dangers of winter

D To entertain readers with a funny story

Jammin' Joe's Hamburgers

Jammin' Joe's has the best hamburgers in the world! They're big and juicy. We top them with cheese, lettuce, tomato, pickles, ketchup, and mustard. They're the best-tasting hamburgers ever! Come to Jammin' Joe's, and try the world's BEST hamburger!

3 What is the main reason the author wrote this passage?

A To teach readers about how to put toppings on hamburgers

B To entertain readers with a story about making a hamburger

C To persuade readers to try a hamburger at Jammin' Joe's

D To share a viewpoint about burgers being the best food ever

The Fastest Animal

What is the fastest animal in the world? Do you know? Many people think it's the cheetah. The cheetah is a wild cat, and it is the fastest on land. But the fastest animal in the world is the peregrine falcon. It is one fast bird! The peregrine falcon can fly faster than 200 miles per hour. It can reach this speed by diving off a cliff to catch bugs and other snacks.

4 What is the author's main reason for writing this passage?

A To persuade the reader to buy a peregrine falcon for a house pet

B To entertain the reader with a story about how peregrine falcons play

C To teach the reader why the peregrine falcon is the fastest animal of all

D To inform the reader how deadly and dangerous the peregrine falcon is

Having Fun in the Sun

When the weather is warm, we all like to be outdoors. If you are playing in the sun, remember some safety tips.

- Put on sunscreen so that you don't get sunburned.
- Make sure you wear shoes that are right for what you're doing.
- If you are running around much of the time, socks and tennis shoes are easier on your feet than sandals.
- Many times, playing outdoors means getting dirty, so wear old clothes…that way, no one will get upset when you come home with stains on them!

5 Now tell it in your own words. What is the main purpose of this passage?

____

____

____

Main Idea

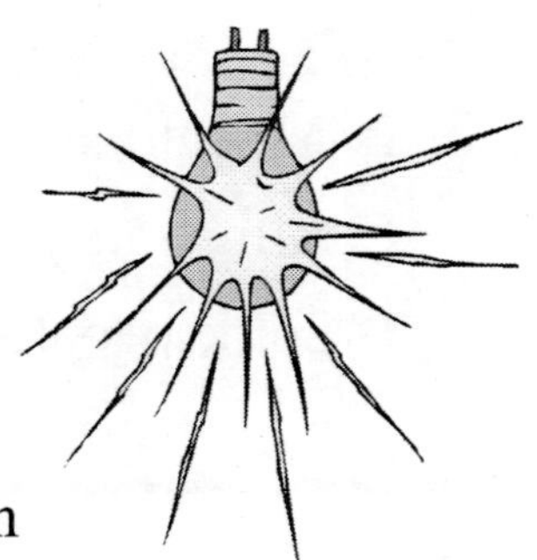

The **main idea** is what a passage is all about. It is the "big idea" of the passage. When you read, ask yourself: "What is this passage about? What is it trying to say?"

Everything you read has a main idea. This is what the text is about. Real stories have main ideas. Made-up stories do too.

It is easy to find the main idea. Sometimes you can find the main idea in the title. For example, read this title.

What I Did for Summer Vacation

What will this passage be about? Most likely, it will tell what the author did over the summer. The title shows the "big idea" of the passage.

Other times, the main idea is a sentence in the passage. This sentence can be at the beginning or at the end of the passage. For example, say you read a passage about baseball. It tells what happens in the game and why it is fun to watch. The last sentence says, "Baseball is a great sport." This sentence tells you that the main idea is how great baseball is.

Now that you know a little more about the main idea, let's practice.

Practice 2: Main Idea

RI 1, 2, **RF** 4 (DOK 2)

DIRECTIONS **Read the passages, and choose the main idea.**

Dangerous Pets

Alligators are dangerous, so they do not make good pets. Some people buy baby alligators and try to keep them as pets. They may be cute when they are little, but they grow fast. As they grow, they need a lot to eat. Adult alligators eat about twenty pounds of meat a week. Their teeth get very sharp. They can hurt their owners. Also, they can ruin a house. As they grow, they need room to move around. They can grow to be around twelve feet long and weigh eight hundred pounds! They get strong and can break out of a cage. Then, they can wreck furniture, floors, and walls. It is not a good idea to have an alligator as a pet.

1 What is the main idea of this passage?

A It's expensive to keep some animals as pets.

B Alligators are dangerous and don't make good pets.

C Alligators grow quickly and their teeth get very sharp.

D Some people buy cute baby alligators and keep them as pets.

Grandma Georgiana

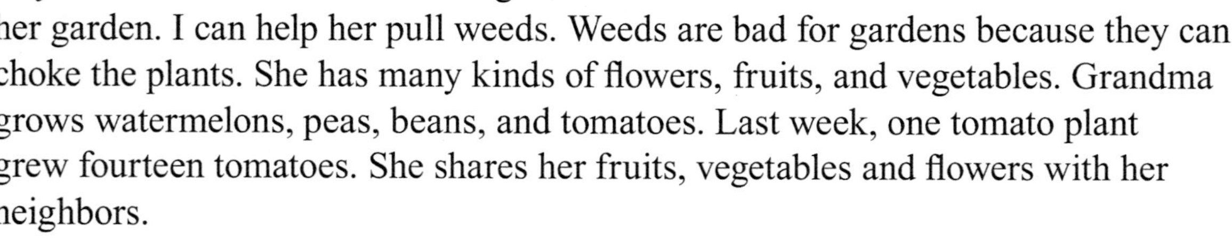

My grandma is a sweet lady. She bakes bread for breakfast on the weekends. She dresses very plainly, by wearing blue pants and a white top. She is pretty with smooth caramel-colored skin and large brown eyes. She has bright eyes and a warm smile.

I do not want to go to school today. I want to stay at home with Grandma Georgiana and work in her garden. I can help her pull weeds. Weeds are bad for gardens because they can choke the plants. She has many kinds of flowers, fruits, and vegetables. Grandma grows watermelons, peas, beans, and tomatoes. Last week, one tomato plant grew fourteen tomatoes. She shares her fruits, vegetables and flowers with her neighbors.

Grandma also walks two miles every day. She takes along her dog, Little Bit. He is a teacup pup because he only weighs two pounds. He could probably fit inside a teacup! Have you ever seen such a tiny dog? While my grandma is walking, she takes a small plastic bag and picks up garbage from the side of the road. She is a good citizen. She helps her family and friends all the time. I love my Grandma Georgiana.

2 What is the main idea of this passage?

A The author does not like going to school.

B The author loves her grandma's dog, Little Bit.

C Grandma Georgiana is kind and interesting.

D Grandma Georgiana bakes delicious bread.

Supporting Details

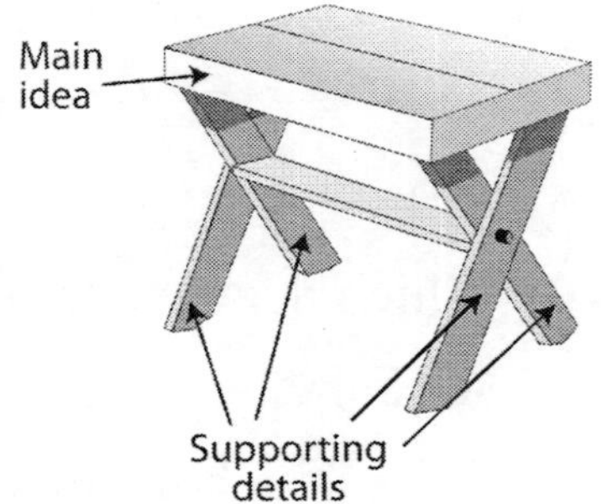

Supporting details tell about the main idea. They are smaller ideas that hold up the main idea. Think about a passage being like a table. The top of the table is the main idea. The details are the legs that hold up the table. They are facts, reasons, and examples that support the main idea. Supporting details make the main idea stronger.

What if your friends said, "We had the best time at Sam's house this weekend"? You would want to know why they had such a good time. The things they did at Sam's house are the supporting details. Read the example below. The supporting details are underlined.

> We had the best time at Sam's house this weekend! <u>We played video games and jumped on the trampoline. Sam's mom made us ice cream sundaes. Later, we watched a movie.</u>

The main idea is "We had the best time at Sam's house." All of the other sentences are supporting details. They explain why Sam's house was so much fun.

Practice 3: Supporting Details

RI 1, 2, **RF** 4, **W** 2, **L** 1, 2, 3.a (DOK 1–3)

A.

DIRECTIONS **Read the passage, and then answer the questions after it.**

Lincoln's Life

Abraham Lincoln was born in a log cabin on February 12, 1809. As a young boy, he learned to work very hard. When he was eight years old, he helped his father build a new log cabin.

He did not go to school long because he had to work on the farm. But he loved to read. By the time he was seventeen, Abe knew he wanted to be a lawyer. He was always fair and honest.

He went on to become our sixteenth president. He was a great president and achieved many things. One of the most important was helping to end slavery.

Chapter 4

1 What is this passage mostly about?

____

____

____

2 Which detail supports the idea that Lincoln was a great president?

A He helped to end slavery.

B He was born in a log cabin.

C He was always fair and honest.

D He loved to read and to learn.

3 Which president did Lincoln grow up to become?

A First
C Sixteenth
B Thirtieth
D Thirteenth

4 What did Lincoln want to be when he grew up?

A Builder
C Doctor
B Lawyer
D Farmer

5 Why did Abe stop going to school?

A His family moved around too much.

B He did enough reading on his own.

C He had to work on the family farm.

D He didn't like going to school much.

6 Why did the author write this passage?

A To inform readers about Lincoln's life

B To show how it pays off to study hard

C To tell what Lincoln was like as a boy

D To entertain readers with a fun story

Abraham Lincoln

B.

DIRECTIONS **Read the passages below. Underline the supporting details in each passage.**

Niagara Falls

Niagara Falls is a beautiful place to visit. It is partly in New York and partly in Canada. There are three waterfalls at Niagara Falls. They are all very big! The biggest one is over 184 feet high.

Sarah Sue's Zoo

Sarah Sue had so many pets that her house looked like a zoo. She had a mouse, a chicken, a pig, a bird, a gerbil, a cat, and a dog. Sometimes the cat would try to eat the mouse or the bird. Sometimes the dog would chase the cat. And sometimes the pig would chase the chicken!

Tide Pools

Tide pools are watery little habitats on the beach. They contain many kinds of animals. Snails, crabs, and fish are some of the living creatures you can find there. Waves crashing on the rocks at the seashore leave water behind. These become pools protected by the surrounding rocks. The pools make homes for all kinds of interesting wildlife.

Niagara Falls

Crab in Tidepool

Sarah Sue's Pets

C.

DIRECTIONS **Read these two passages. Both give some facts that are similar. They also talk about ideas that are not alike.**

1 Underline the sentences in both passages that show how the ideas are alike. The first one in each passage is done for you.

Soccer

Soccer is a great sport to play. Soccer players have to learn how to kick and pass the ball. The goalie has to learn how to stop the ball. Playing soccer helps to give you athletic stamina and energy. Without these, it would be hard to compete. Every soccer player must learn how to control the ball. Most importantly, each player has to work with others as a team.

Swimming

Swimming is great exercise. It is one of the healthiest exercises anyone can do. Swimming helps to build your stamina and energy. It also makes your muscles strong. The key is to keep moving in the water. Swimmers have to learn to take quick breaths. Then they need to hold their breath under the water. This helps your lungs get strong. Besides being fun, swimming is good exercise for the whole body.

2 Both passages are about a sport or exercise. But what is different about them? What are the main ways that soccer and swimming are not alike? Use examples from what you read.

____

____

____

Practice 4: Writing to Inform or Explain

RI 1, 2, **RF** 4, **W** 2, 4, 10, **L** 1–6 (DOK 3)

In the last practice, you read about a place (Niagara Falls), some animals (a cat, crabs, snails, and so on), and a person (Sarah Sue). Now, choose a place, animal, or person that you know.

DIRECTIONS

Write about the place, animal, or person you picked. Describe your subject so that your readers can picture what you are writing about. Use your own paper to write your essay. Make sure your writing is clear and has a beginning, middle, and end.

Activity

W 5, **SL** 1.a–d, 4, 6

In a small group or in class, read your essay about the place, animal, or person you chose. Ask other students to tell what questions they have about it.

For example, say that you wrote about your pet fish. You might tell what you named it, what color it is, how often you feed it, and so on. But someone might ask, "How many fins does your fish have?"

People asking questions can help you see what you left out. Make notes about what people ask you. Then revise your essay to add what they asked about.

Chapter 4 Summary

Informational text is nonfiction writing that gives you facts and tells about real people, places, and events.

The **author's purpose** is the reason why an author writes. Here are some reasons why an author might write a text:

- to entertain
- to inform
- to teach
- to persuade (convince)
- to share a viewpoint

When you read, think about **your own point of view** and whether or not you agree with the author.

The **main idea** is what the passage is about. It is the "big idea" of the passage.

Supporting details are the facts, reasons, and examples that explain the main idea.

For more practice with this chapter's material, see the Informational Texts Review on page 93.

Chapter 5
Understand What You Read

This chapter covers DOK levels 1–3 and the following third grade strands and standards (for full standards, please see Appendix A):

Reading Literature: 7, 9, 10

Reading Informational Texts: 1, 3, 5, 7–10

Reading Foundational Skills: 4

Writing: 1, 2, 4–6, 8, 10

Speaking and Listening: 4–6

Language: 1, 3, 6

When you read a book or article, you need to know what it is about. There are many ways to understand what you read. This chapter will give you helpful hints for how to get the most out of your reading.

Read Carefully

Sometimes you might have to read a long article. You may not have time to read every single word. So how can you know what the article is about? You can look closely at what you read without reading every word.

Skimming gives you an overview. When you skim, you look over a passage. You get a general idea of what it is about. You read the title and any section headers. It is a good idea to read the first paragraph and the last one. You can also read the first sentence of the other paragraphs.

Scanning helps you find specific ideas. When you scan, you look for words and phrases. These might be in a question you need to answer. Scanning is most helpful after you have already read a passage.

When reading, it's also important to practice **raising questions**. This means asking yourself questions about what you read. As you look at the passage, try to answer the questions you thought of. It is helpful to use the **five Ws and one H**: *who*, *what*, *where*, *why*, *when*, and *how*.

Practice 1: Read Carefully

RI 1, 10, **RF** 4 (DOK 1)

DIRECTIONS **Read the passage, and answer the questions.**

Busy Otters

Otters are small animals. They have to eat a lot. This is because they are very busy. Otters know how to dig and swim well. An otter can swim under water for eight minutes! Otters like to play in snow. Some even like to race down hills. They can run quickly. They are able to catch lots of bugs. Otters are also good at catching fish. Otters do many things!

1 According to the passage, how long can an otter hold its breath under water?

A Three minutes

B Five minutes

C Eight minutes

D Ten minutes

2 What do otters like to chase?

A Rolling snowballs

B Cars and bikes

C Falling snowflakes

D Bugs and fish

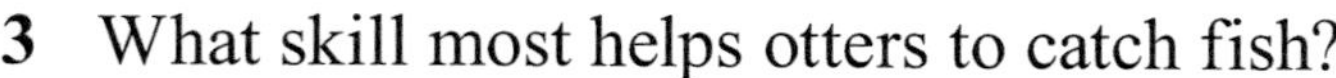

3 What skill most helps otters to catch fish?

A They can swim fast.

B They like the snow.

C They race each other.

D They can catch bugs.

Events in a Passage

One way to understand a passage is to look at *when* events in it happen. When authors write, they use a **sequence of events**. This is also called **time order**. Both fiction and nonfiction passages use sequence. Sequence of events can go from the first to the last event. Other times, it goes from last to first. Sometimes it can jump around!

It is important to see how events relate to each other. You should be able to tell the order in which things happen. As you read, you will see clues about the order of events. Here is an example.

> I stepped up to the plate and dug my cleat into the dirt. Before moving into position, I looked around at my teammates at first and second base. Then I tapped the home plate three times with my bat for good luck. Bringing the bat into position, I eyed the pitcher, and he eyed me. Finally, he pitched. Keeping my eye on the ball the best I could, I swung with all my might. In a flash, I heard a sound that was music to my ears: "crack!"

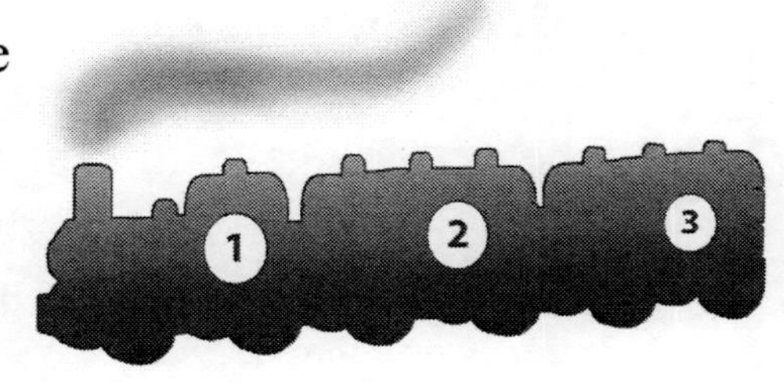

The passage tells about a baseball player's turn at bat. The sequence moves in time order. Words like "Then" and "Finally" give you clues about when events happen. The word "Before" also gives an important clue. It shows that two events happen out of order. First, the batter looks around at teammates on the bases. Second, the batter moves into position. When you read, watch for these kinds of clue words. You can even make a story map to follow the order of events. (See the example on page 194.)

Sequence is important in other ways. It needs to be correct to show a process. For example, it must be in the right order for a science experiment. Directions also must be in the right order. And you need the right sequence to follow a recipe.

Cause and Effect

Another way to understand what is in a passage is to look at *why* events happen. Many events have a **cause-effect relationship**.

- A **cause** is the reason why something happens.
- An **effect** is the result. Look at the example below:

Cause: heavy rain

Effect: flooding

In this example, heavy rain causes flooding. Heavy rain is the cause. Flooding is the effect.

When you know how events relate to each other, you can understand a passage better. Making a fishbone map like the one on page 195 will help you figure out causes and effects as you read a text.

Practice 2: Events in a Passage

RI 1, 3, 8, 10, **RF** 4 (DOK 1, 3)

DIRECTIONS **Read the passage, and answer the questions.**

Sir Francis Drake

Sir Francis Drake was a famous English explorer. He sailed the seas to find new ways to get places. He was born in 1540 and died in 1596. Drake was the second explorer ever to circumnavigate the globe. That means he went around the whole world in a ship. The first person to do that was Ferdinand Magellan, about fifty years earlier.

In Drake's time, England and Spain were enemies. So the Queen of England asked Drake to help beat the Spanish. She knew he was the best at sailing and knew the sea. She gave him ships to use and money for his voyages. Drake made a job out of bothering Spanish ships at sea. He stole from them when he could. In this way, he was also a pirate. Drake spent much of his life at sea.

1 When was Sir Francis Drake born?

A 1596 **B** 1540 **C** 1600 **D** 1659

2 How many people had sailed around the world before Drake?

A 1 **B** 2 **C** 5 **D** 6

3 Which event happened first?

A Drake became a pirate.

B Drake sailed around the globe.

C Drake found new ways to get places.

D Drake worked for the Queen of England.

4 How did the Queen of England know that Drake was very good at sailing the seas?

____

____

____

Landslides

Sometimes it rains so much that the earth moves! If it rains a lot in a short amount of time, the ground gets soaked. The hard ground turns into soft mud. In very hilly areas, this wet ground can result in a landslide. When this happens, mud starts to flow down a hillside. The landslide moves faster and faster as it goes down the steep hill. It picks up more dirt, mud, and rocks as it moves along. This makes the landslide grow. It is similar to the way a snowball gets bigger when you roll it in the snow. Landslides can cause bad damage. People should have an emergency plan ready if they think there might be landslides in their area.

5 What is the main cause of landslides?

A A hillside

B Heavy rain

C Flat land

D People

6 What happens as a landslide moves down a hill?

____

____

____

Chopsticks

Many people like Asian food. Some eat it with chopsticks. They use chopsticks instead of a knife and fork. Chopsticks are two thin sticks. They can be made of wood or plastic.

Using chopsticks may look easy, but it takes practice. You have to hold them just right. First, you hold the bottom one like you would hold a pencil. The top stick fits right above it. You only move the top one up and down with your first finger. This looks like you are pinching the air.

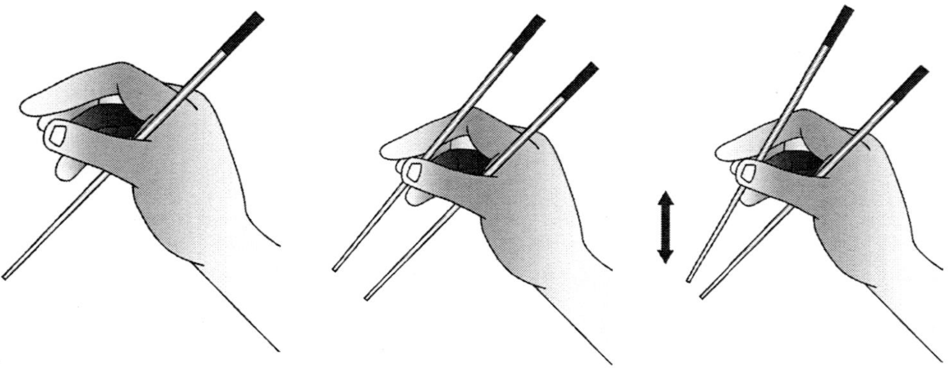

Practice that motion for a while. Then try to pick up a piece of food. Be patient. It will take some time. But don't give up! It's fun to do.

7 Why does the author say people should try using chopsticks?

A Many people like the challenge.

B You can't eat Asian food with a fork.

C Chopsticks are easier to find than silverware.

D It is a lot of fun to eat with chopsticks.

8 How does the illustration help you understand the text?

___

___

___

Compare and Contrast

One way to respond to what you read is to **compare and contrast** parts of it. You can also compare and contrast two different texts about the same topic. To compare means to look at how things are alike. To contrast means to look at how they are different.

Venn diagrams are used to help us compare and contrast. You can make your own by following the example on page 195.

You can compare and contrast two texts. Think about what happens in both. Also, look at where they take place. Say you read two texts that are both set in outer space. One is about a real NASA mission. The other is a made-up story about aliens coming to Earth. As you can see, the two stories would be alike in some ways. They would be very different in other ways.

Did you know that stories can be like real life? They can, even if they are made up! Even with talking animals, the events might be like things that can happen to you. Read this passage from a story.

> Travis the Turtle walked down the lane, searching up and down. He stumbled. He got turned around. His feet were sore from all the walking he was doing. He was crying a little because he was scared and tired. Where was the corner of the field that he knew? Where was the path that led to his house?

Which is most similar to what happens in the story about Travis?

A A boy gets lost while shopping with his mother.

B A girl misplaces her bike and has to walk home.

C A family finds a turtle in a field near their house.

D A farmer plows his field, and it looks different.

Did you pick A? That's right. Travis may be a turtle, but he is lost in this story. So, the experience of a boy who gets lost is most similar to that.

Practice 3: Compare and Contrast

RI 1, 8, 9 (DOK 1–3)

DIRECTIONS **Read the passage. Then answer the questions about it.**

Ratatouille takes place in Paris, France. The main character is a rat, and he can talk. His name is Remy. He helps a new chef. The chef does not cook very well. Remy helps him make delicious meals. He enjoys cooking and loves fine food even though he is just a rat.

Madeline is also set in Paris. Madeline is a little girl. She lives at a school with other girls. She is the smallest, but she is brave and spunky! One day, she has to go to the hospital. She has her appendix taken out. She gets gifts and flowers. The other girls are jealous.

1 What is most similar about these two stories?

A What happens in the stories

B The two main characters

C Where the stories take place

D The ending of both stories

2 How is Remy most different from Madeline?

____

____

____

3 Which experience is most similar to Remy's experience?

A A horse with a hurt leg gets better, and he learns to run and jump again.

B A boy from a tropical country wants to ski and becomes a skiing teacher.

C A girl dreams of becoming a singer, and one day she wins a talent contest.

D A spider spins a web that gets washed away by rain, but she spins it again.

4 Which experience is most similar to Madeline's?

A A boy falls from a tree and gets a cast put on his leg. All his friends sign the cast. Now each of his friends wants a cast too.

B A dog has puppies. There are several of them. One is the smallest, but he is very active. He's fun to play with.

C A group of children lives at a school. They play together and go on adventures. They have a nice teacher too.

D A family takes a trip to France. They see all the famous places and buildings. They even go up in the Eiffel Tower.

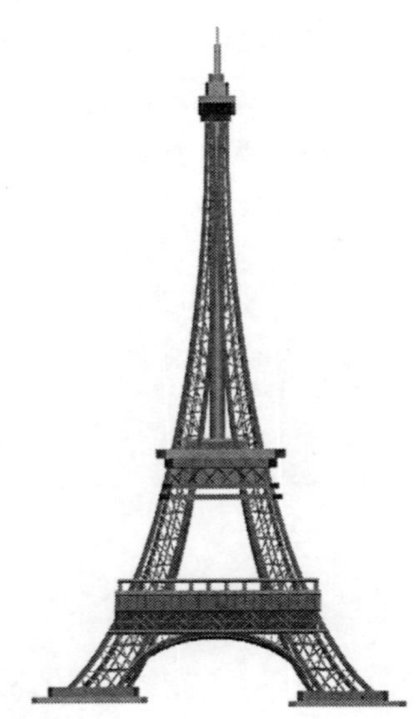

Text Features

There are many **text features** that can help you find information. They also help you better understand what you read.

Text Features in Print

Some books and articles have **headings**. You will see them just above paragraphs. They let you know what you are about to read. Some books also have a **table of contents** to help you locate a certain topic.

For example, say you are reading a book titled *Gorillas: Gentle Giants of the Forest.* In which of these chapters would you look for what gorillas eat?

Chapter	Page
Myths about Gorillas	5
The Diet of Gorillas	11
Where Gorillas Live	13
Gorilla Communication	16

If you chose "The Diet of Gorillas," you are correct! The table of contents in the book has all the chapter names. Looking at this list can help you find what you need.

Sidebars or **text boxes** have extra information. They are boxes of text next to the main text. Many times you see them in magazine or newspaper articles. They have facts that relate to the main passage.

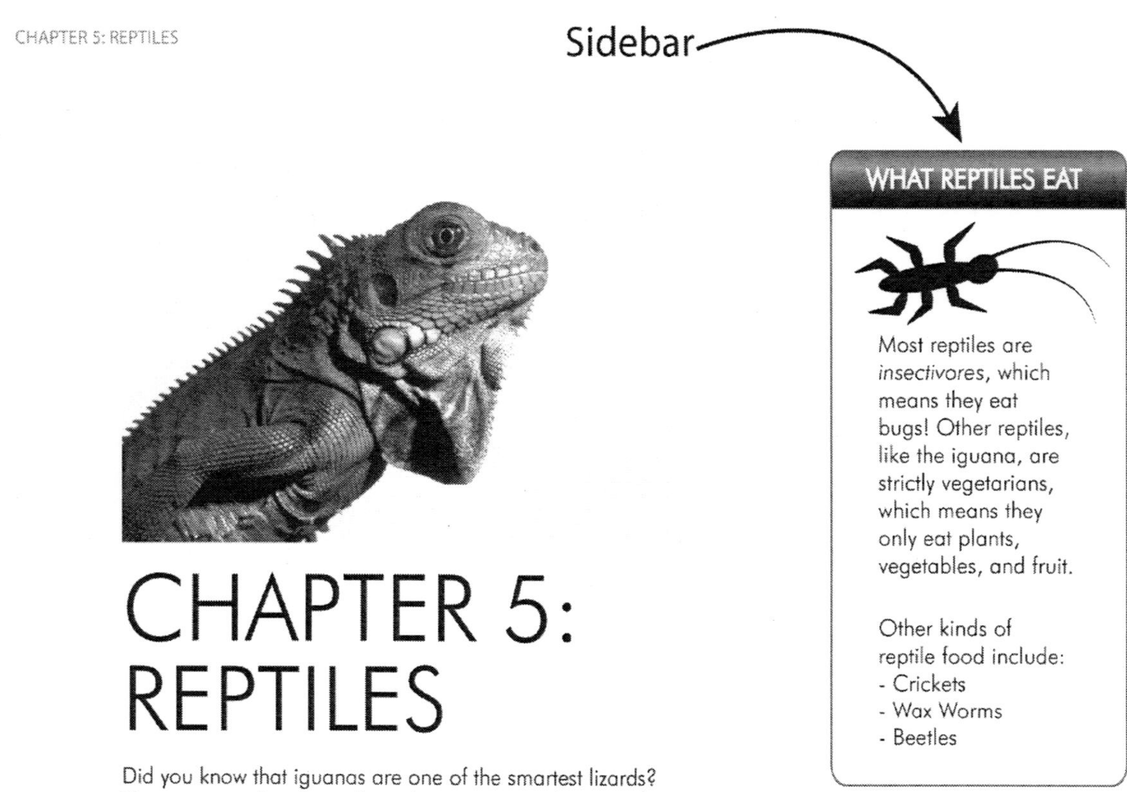

CHAPTER 5: REPTILES
Sidebar
WHAT REPTILES EAT
Most reptiles are insectivores, which means they eat bugs! Other reptiles, like the iguana, are strictly vegetarians, which means they only eat plants, vegetables, and fruit.
Other kinds of reptile food include:
- Crickets
- Wax Worms
- Beetles
CHAPTER 5: REPTILES
Did you know that iguanas are one of the smartest lizards? They require a lot of care from their owners and are very hard to keep as pets. Before getting an iguana, you should take into consideration some of the following facts about keeping an iguana in your house:

Text Features on the Internet

At times, you will use the Internet to find information. The best way to find a topic is to use a search engine. Some examples are Google, Yahoo!, and MSN. Each has a space where you can type in your topic. To find your topic, you type in a **key word**. Key words should be specific. Say that you need to do a report about a type of dog. You decide your dog will be a boxer. If you use the key word *boxer*, you will get millions of pages! Some will be about the dog, but others may be about the sport of boxing. Some may even be sites that sell boxer shorts! So be specific. Try *boxer dog* instead.

As you search, you will see another feature. It is called a **hyperlink**. It appears in special type. Often it is another color and underlined. Clicking on it takes you to another webpage. Pages on the Internet often link to each other.

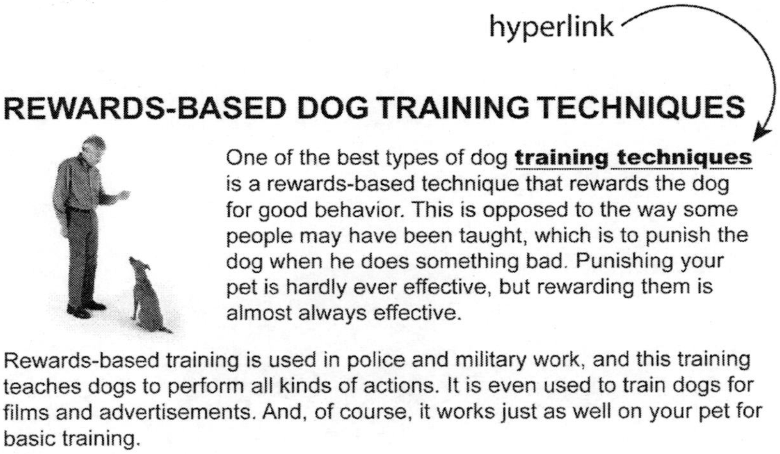

hyperlink

REWARDS-BASED DOG TRAINING TECHNIQUES

One of the best types of dog **training techniques** is a rewards-based technique that rewards the dog for good behavior. This is opposed to the way some people may have been taught, which is to punish the dog when he does something bad. Punishing your pet is hardly ever effective, but rewarding them is almost always effective.

Rewards-based training is used in police and military work, and this training teaches dogs to perform all kinds of actions. It is even used to train dogs for films and advertisements. And, of course, it works just as well on your pet for basic training.

You also see sidebars on the Internet. They often contain links to other pages. The left sidebar on a webpage might be like a table of contents.

GRAPHICS

Another text feature is **graphics**. You will see graphics in printed books and on the Internet. They can be **illustrations** (drawings), **maps**, **photographs**, or **charts**. Graphics help you better understand the text.

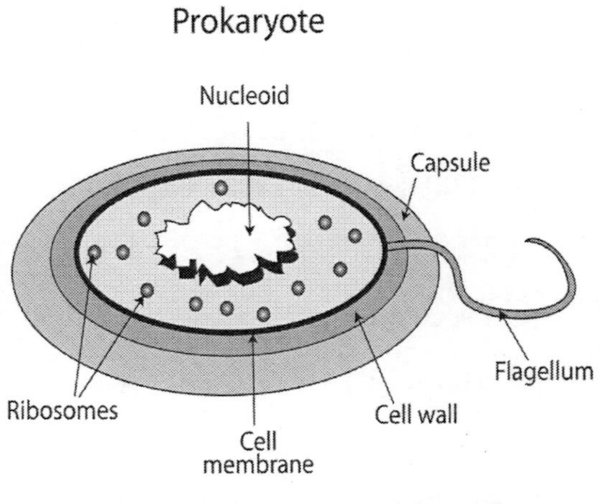

In stories, **illustrations** can help create a mood. They can also show you how a character or setting looks.

Prokaryote

Nucleoid
Capsule
Flagellum
Ribosomes
Cell wall
Cell membrane

Graphic Showing Parts of a Cell

A **chart** helps to put things in order. It might be a way to look at how many things there are. Or, it can help you see what happens over time. A chart also can compare two or more things.

For example, a pie chart is a way to show parts of a whole. It can tell you, "How many?" Amanda asked ten friends what state they were born in. The whole pie is all of her ten friends. Each piece is a part of the whole group. It shows what they said.

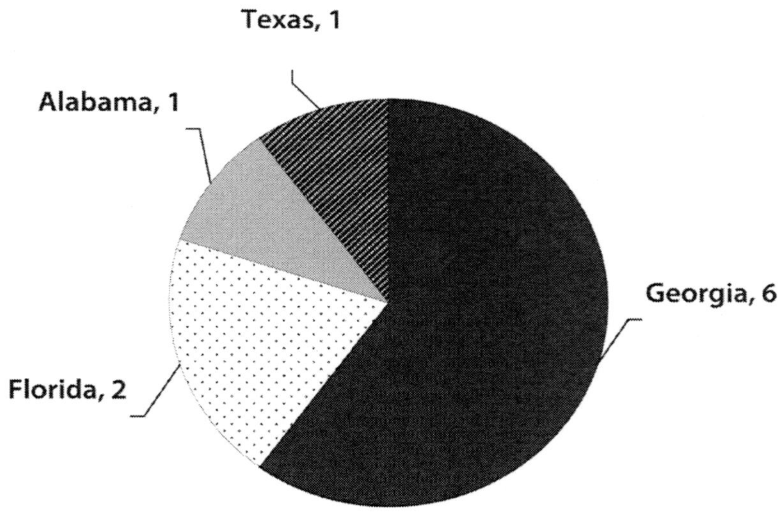

Where were most of Amanda's friends born?

A Alabama

B Florida

C Georgia

D Texas

Did you pick C? You are right! You can tell because the slice that shows Georgia is the biggest.

A **map** shows where places are. You can use it to find your way. Maps can show big areas like a continent or the whole world. They can also show more specific places. For example, when you go to the mall, a map shows where each store is located.

Practice 4: Text Features

RI 5 (DOK 1–3)

DIRECTIONS **Answer the questions that follow.**

1 Say you are doing a report about how mountain climbing got started. You want to look for facts on the Internet. What would be the best key word to use?

A mountain climbing

B climbing how it started

C climbing equipment

D mountain climbing history

2 Look at the sample table of contents below. Answer the question that follows.

Table of Contents	
Our Universe by Chase Lightner	
Chapter 1 Introduction.	1
The Universe.	8
Solar Systems.	10
Chapter 2 Our Solar System	11
The Sun	12
Mercury	14
Venus	16
Earth	18
Earth's Moon	20
Mars	22
Jupiter	26
Saturn	28
Uranus	30
Neptune	32
Chapter 3 Studying Space	35
Astronomers	36
Telescopes	42
Space Probes	47

Chapter 5

In which chapter would you find information about the Hubble Space Telescope?

____

3 On which page does the section about Saturn begin?

____

4 If you wanted to find information about the age of the universe, on which page would you begin to look?

____

DIRECTIONS **Read this passage. Then answer the questions.**

I went to camp last week. It was not a sleep-away camp. I was there all day, but I came home every night. It was fun. We made cool things! This is the schedule they gave us. We got to pick what we wanted to do. I made a little plane out of balsa wood. I made a scary mask too. My mom most liked the picture of trees and a lake that I painted.

9:00 a.m. Check in
10:00 a.m. Welcome session
10:30 a.m. Craft A (choose from table below)
12:00 p.m. Lunch
1:00 p.m. Craft B (choose from table below)
2:30 p.m. Craft C (choose from table below)
4:00 p.m. Free time to play

Craft A	Craft B	Craft C
Jewelry Making Model Airplanes Sock Puppets	Kites Masks Clay Shaping	Paper Dolls Finger Painting Drawing Cartoons

5 What activity would a child who likes to sketch most likely choose?

A Jewelry Making

B Sock Puppets

C Drawing Cartoons

D Clay Shaping

6 According to the passage, what three activities did the author do?

____

____

____

7 If you went to this camp, what time could you learn to make a kite?

A 10:30 a.m.

B 1:00 p.m.

C 2:30 p.m.

D 4:00 p.m.

8 The author will present a speech in class about his time at camp. What would be the best graphic to help the audience understand the speech?

____

____

____

Practice 5: Writing about What You Read or Saw

RI 1, 3, 10, **RFS** 4, **W** 1, 2, 8, 10, **L** 1–6 (DOK 3)

DIRECTIONS

Write about the last book you read or movie you saw.

- **Briefly tell about the events in it. Make sure the sequence is clear.**
- **Tell what you thought of it. Include ideas from the book or film to support your opinion.**
- **Make sure your writing is clear and has a beginning, middle, and end.**
- **Finally, choose an illustration that will help people to understand your essay better.**

Activity

SL 2, 4, 5

After writing your essay for Practice 5, make a speech out of it. Give a presentation about your book or movie to the class or to a small group of students. Make your speech fun to listen to. Be sure to speak clearly. Include words that show the order of events. Save a few minutes at the end to answer any questions from your audience.

You can also make an audio recording of your speech. Record your voice using CD, tape, or digital audio. Listen to your presentation. Is it interesting? Do you talk at a speed that is easy to follow? Will people understand what you say? Fix anything you need to. Then record it again.

Chapter 5 Summary

Most of the time, you will **read carefully**. Sometimes you can look closely at what you read without reading every word.

Skimming gives you an overview of the topic.

Scanning helps you find specific information in a passage.

Raising questions means asking yourself questions about what you read and trying to answer them.

A **sequence of events** is the order that events happen. This is also called **time order**.

Many events have a **cause-effect relationship**. A **cause** is the reason why something happens. An **effect** is the result.

You can **compare and contrast** stories and everything in them.

Text features can help you find information. In printed texts, they include the **table of contents**, **headings**, **sidebars**, and **text boxes**. On the Internet, they include **key words**, **hyperlinks**, and **sidebars**.

Graphics in a printed book and on the Internet help you understand the text. They can be **illustrations** (drawings), **maps**, **photographs**, or **charts**.

For further review of this chapter's material, see the Informational Texts Review on page 93.

Informational Texts Review

This chapter covers DOK levels 1–3 and the following third grade strands and standards (for full standards, please see Appendix A):

Reading Literature: 7, 10
Reading Informational Texts: 1–10
Reading Foundational Skills: 4
Writing: 1, 2, 4–8, 10
Speaking and Listening: 1–6
Language: 1– 3, 6

This review will give you more practice with the skills you read about in chapters 4 and 5.

DIRECTIONS **First, read the passages. Answer the questions that follow. Then, you will write about what you read.**

The Water Cycle

Clouds form when there is water in the sky. Water from the ground gets pulled back up into the sky. This is called evaporation.

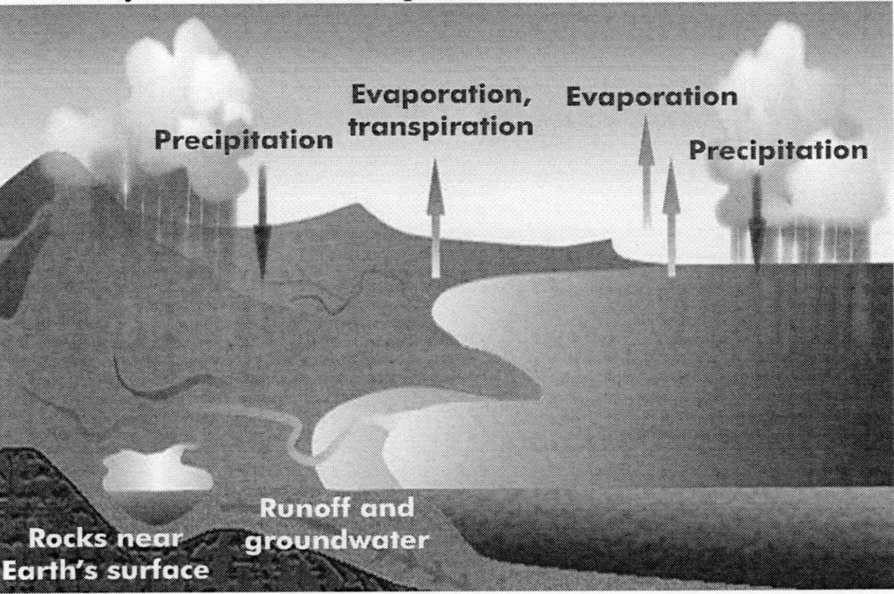

Evaporation

Evaporation is when a liquid changes to a gas form. Water becomes vapor. This happens faster in warmer places. For example, think about a cup of water standing on a table. It might take a week or two for all the water to evaporate. But you could boil the same amount of water in a pot on the stove. It would turn to vapor in minutes.

Transpiration

Plants get water from the soil. The water moves from the roots up to the stems. It winds up in the leaves. From the leaves, some of it evaporates into the air. Where there are many plants and trees, like in forests, a large amount of water transpires into the air.

Condensation

When the water cools, it becomes clouds. This is called condensation. Clouds are made of tiny droplets of water. When they gather in the sky, you can see them in the form of clouds.

Types of Clouds

Stratus clouds are very thick. They are flat clouds that stay close to the ground. If stratus clouds touch the ground, they are known as fog.

Cumulus clouds are big, white, and puffy. They are not very high in the sky. When these clouds fill up with rain, they might turn dark and gray.

Cirrus clouds are thin, wispy clouds. They are really high in the sky. These clouds can come after a storm.

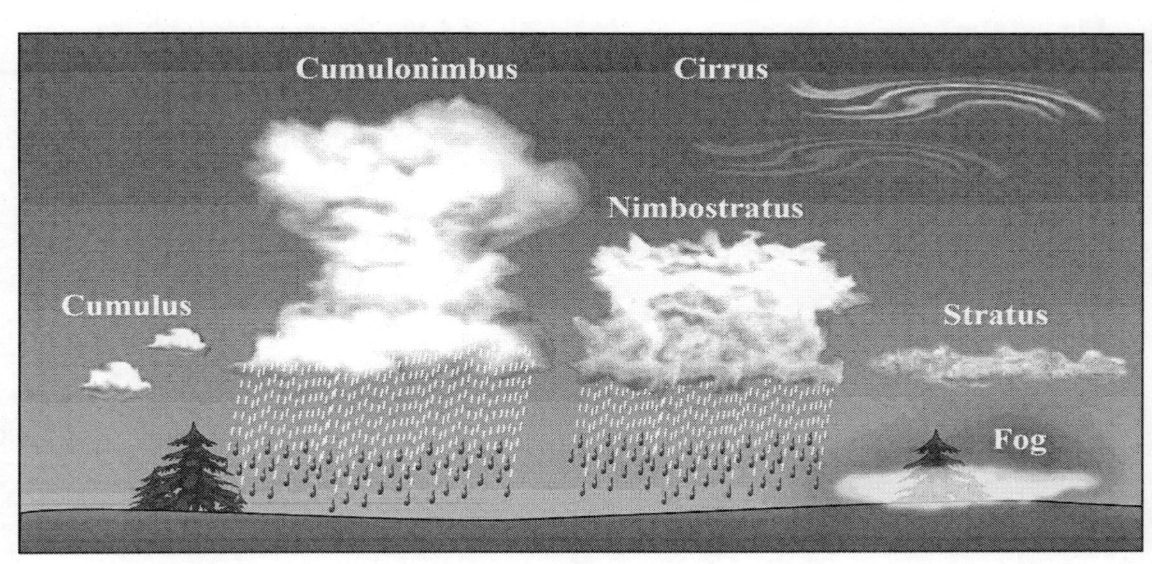

Precipitation

When the droplets get too big to stay up in the sky, they fall back to the earth as rain and snow. This is called precipitation. There are several kinds of clouds. Certain kinds of clouds produce rain or snow. Once the water falls back to the earth, the process begins all over again.

Practice 1: The Water Cycle

RI 1–10, **RF** 4, **L** 1– 3, 6

DIRECTIONS **Answer these questions about the passage you just read.**

1

DOK 3

What is the main idea of the passage?

____

____

____

2 DOK 2

Why did the author write this passage?

A To show readers how rain helps plants to grow

B To educate readers about how water moves around

C To inform readers about different kinds of clouds

D To entertain readers with a story about water vapor

3 DOK 1

What is the best way to describe cumulus clouds?

A They are big, white, and puffy like cotton candy.

B They are high clouds that fill with rain and get dark.

C They are very high in the sky and pretty to look at.

D They are low, white clouds that get dark before it rains.

4 DOK 2

What most helps you to tell what each paragraph is about?

A The last sentence in each paragraph

B The subheading of each paragraph

C The first word in each paragraph

D The title of the whole article

5 DOK 1

Look at the illustration of different clouds. Based on this, which types of clouds make rain and snow?

A Cumulonimbus and nimbostratus

B Stratus and cumulonimbus

C Cumulus and nimbostratus

D Cirrus and cumulus

6 DOK 3

It rains less in the desert than it does in places with many plants and trees. Why is that?

____

____

7

DOK 1

Which step of the water cycle would go in the blank?

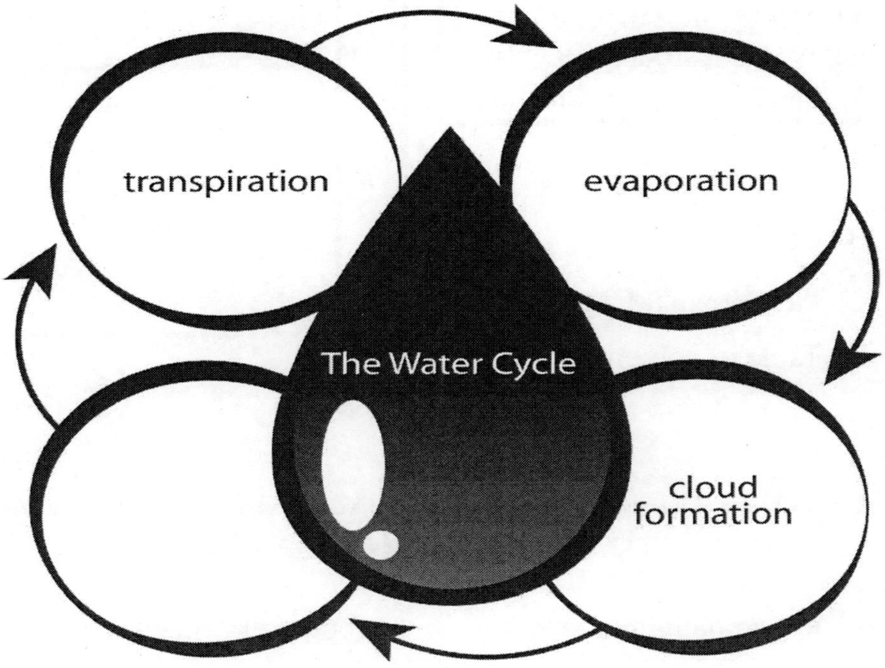

A Cumulonimbus

B Runoff

C Precipitation

D Vapor

8

DOK 3

Why are facts about different clouds in a text box?

____

____

____

9 DOK 2

This passage is from a book about weather. Where in the book would a student look to find the chapter about storms?

A Title page

B Glossary

C Passage headings

D Table of contents

10 DOK 1

What makes water evaporate faster?

A Heat

B Wind

C Plants

D Oceans

To Rain or Not to Rain

by Aesop

A man had two daughters. He loved them both very much.

The older sister became a farmer. The man went to visit his oldest daughter and asked about her farm.

She said, "Everything is fine, but I wish it would rain more often. It would be easier to grow crops if we had more rain."

The man also visited his younger daughter. She was a tile-maker. He asked her how her business was doing.

She replied, "Business is great, and I have only one wish. I hope this dry weather continues and the sun keeps shining. It really helps the tiles dry well."

He said to her, "If your sister hopes for rain and you for dry weather, which am I supposed to hope for?"

Practice 2: To Rain or Not to Rain

RL 7, 10, **RI** 1, 2, 6, 10, **RF** 4

DIRECTIONS **Answer these questions about the passage you just read.**

1 DOK 1

Why does the older sister hope for more rain?

____

____

____

2 DOK 1

Why does the younger sister hope for less rain?

____

____

____

3 DOK 2

The author wrote this passage mainly —

A to inform readers about the region's climate.

B to show that it is hard to please everyone.

C to describe how hard it is to be a farmer.

D to encourage readers to watch the weather.

4 DOK 2

Say that you are telling this story to the class. What would be the best visual to show?

A A picture of a farm during a rainstorm

B A graph of how much rain falls each month

C Charts of how well each business does

D Illustrations of farming and tile-making

5

DOK 3

If you were the father, what would you suggest to your daughters? Why?

____

____

6

DOK 2

Say that you are doing a report about where rain comes from. You want to use one of these passages as a resource. Which question should you ask yourself when deciding which one to use?

A Which passage is more fun to read?

B Which passage explains why it rains?

C Which passage tells why rain is important?

D Which passage has more interesting characters?

Practice 3: Give Your Opinion

W 1, 2, 4–8, 10, **L** 1–6 (DOK 3)

DIRECTIONS **Water is vital for life. Of course, we need to drink it to live. But it also keeps us clean. It helps grow our food. It also allows us to get from one place to another. Write about why water is so important. Your topic might be something about water pollution. Or it could be about conserving water (not using as much). It might even be about how much water people should drink each day.**

Write about the topic you choose. Tell your opinion about it in a clear way. Readers should be able to tell how you feel. Support your opinion. Use facts you find out or already know about your topic.

Use your own paper to write your essay. Make sure your writing is clear and has a beginning, middle, and end. Be clear and descriptive.

Practice 4: Research Project

RL 10, **RI** 10, **RF** 4, **W** 2, 7, 8, 10, **L** 1– 3, 6 (DOK 3)

DIRECTIONS

Do some research about a topic related to water. You can use books and the Internet for your research. Think about topics in science, social studies, or the arts. Here are a few ideas. You also can come up with your own.

Pick the topic you want to write about. Do some research about it. Ask your teacher or the media specialist about the best places to look. Take notes about what you find. Then, write a report about your topic. Make sure it gives facts in a logical order. Give it a beginning, middle, and end. Add supporting details so people will understand your ideas. As a last step, make sure there are no mistakes in it.

Possible Research Topics

Science

- How salt or sugar affects water freezing
- The best way to water plants
- How a water fountain works

Social studies

- How aqueducts work and who used them
- Why the first cities were built on rivers
- How explorers learned to navigate the seas

Arts

- Water in art (for example, artists who paint the ocean)
- The invention of watercolors

Activity

W 2.a, 4, 8 L 1.a–d, 3, 4

Make a diary of all the ways you use water. Use a small notebook, or make a book out of construction paper and yarn. Then, keep track of how you use water. Describe each time you use water. Include details so readers can see what you did. Then, draw a picture of each event. Soon you will have a colorful diary of all the ways you use water!

Share your water diary with classmates. Compare and contrast. How does each person use water? Ask questions about each other's diary.

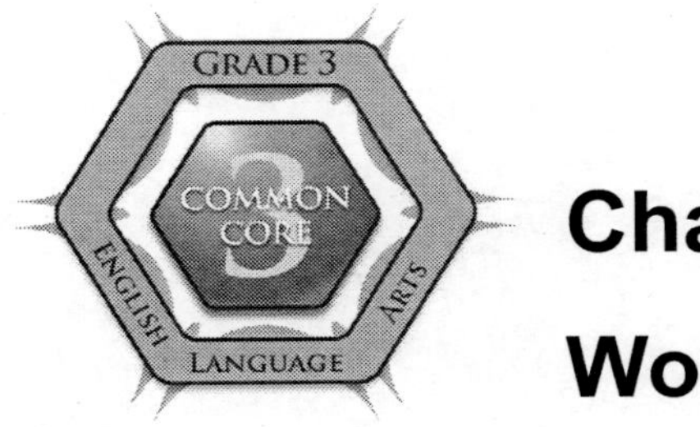

Chapter 6
Word Meaning

This chapter covers DOK levels 2–3 and the following third grade strands and standards (for full standards, please see Appendix A):

Reading Foundational Skills: 3.c, 4.c
Language: 4–6

All the words used in a language are called **vocabulary**. There are many words in the English language. It has a large vocabulary. You should learn as many words as you can. This will help you read and write better.

In this chapter, we will talk about learning new words. We will also discuss using those words. This includes spelling them correctly.

Word Meaning

You may see words you don't know. Don't worry. You're not alone. There are thousands of words out there. No one knows the meaning of all of them. But you can figure out the meaning of new words. Even without a dictionary, there are ways to figure out words.

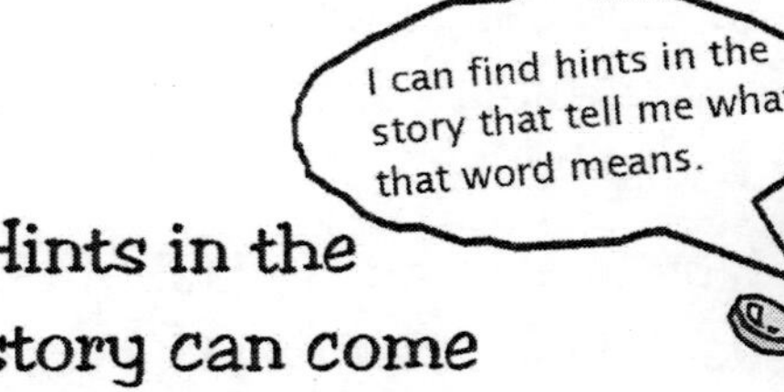

Hints in the story can come before or after a word.

Context Clues

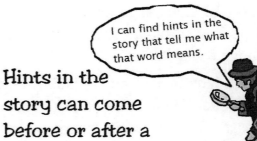

One of the best ways to figure out new words is to use **context clues**. *Context* means what's around something. When you see a word you do not know, look at the words around it. This helps you to understand what the word means. Context clues give you hints about the meaning of a new word.

Look at this example:

The hike was arduous.

Look at the word *arduous*. You may not know what this word means. Looking at it by itself doesn't tell you much about it. It could mean that the hike was fun. Or it could mean that the hike was scary. It could mean almost anything if you don't know the word.

Now, look at the word in context:

> We walked a long way. The trail went up a steep hill. The hike was arduous. I had to stop and rest before walking again.

The words around the word *arduous* are the context clues. Can you figure out what *arduous* means now? Based on the clues, we can guess that *arduous* means "hard" or "difficult."

When you're not sure what a word means, look at the words around the new word for clues. Now that you know a little more about context clues, let's practice.

Syllables

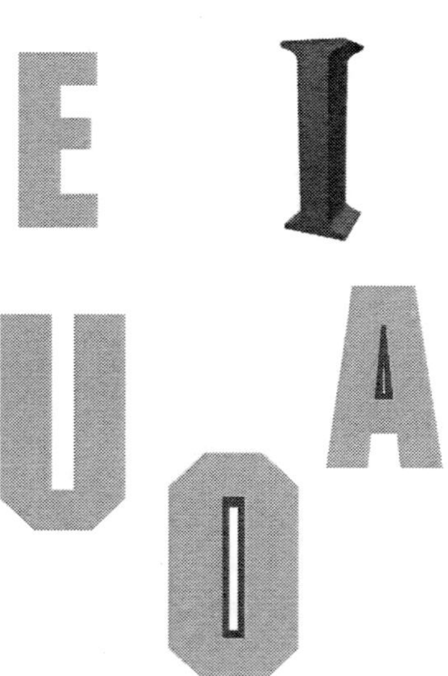

Syllables are chunks of sound. Each syllable has one vowel sound. Look in a mirror as you say words. See how many times your mouth opens? Each time it opens, you are saying one syllable.

All words have at least one syllable. Some have many. If you read one syllable at a time, you can read long words more easily. Here are some examples:

One syllable: word, dog, walked

(Look at the last word, *walked*. It has two vowels, but you only open your mouth once.)

Two syllables: darted, grumble, modern

Three syllables: assistant, languages, Internet

Same Word, Many Meanings

Some words have **multiple meanings**. They always look the same, but they can mean more than one thing. It depends on how they are used. Remember to look at the context.

For example, think about the word *running*. It can be used in several ways.

Examples:

Is the refrigerator running?

Syrup is running off my plate.

Jason is running to catch the bus.

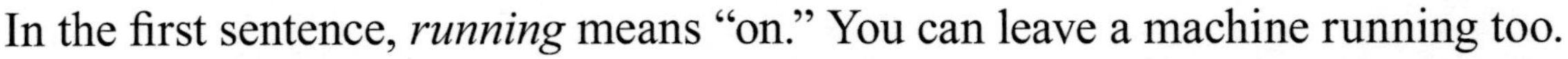

In the first sentence, *running* means "on." You can leave a machine running too.

In the second sentence, *running* means "spilling over." You might have chocolate milk running down your chin!

In the third sentence, *running* means "to move faster than walking, with only one foot at a time touching the ground."

Figurative Language

Authors can use words in exciting ways. They try to paint pictures for readers with the words they use. They do this by saying things in ways you might not expect. This is called **figurative language**.

Figurative Language		
Imagery	Imagery is writing that appeals to the five senses. The words describe how things feel, taste, sound, look, and smell.	**Example:** "During the whole of a dull, dark, and soundless day in the autumn of the year. . ." – Edgar Allan Poe
Metaphor	A metaphor compares things directly, without using *like* or *as*.	**Example:** His smile was a ray of sunshine.
Simile	A simile compares two unlike things using *like* or *as*.	**Example:** He is as happy as a puppy with a new chew toy.
Personification	Personification means to give human qualities to something which is not human.	**Example:** The sun smiled down on us cheerfully.

Figures of speech are made up to help you see in new ways. They do not always mean exactly what they say. Your friend might tell you, "My little brother is a pig! His room is always messy." It does not mean that the boy is an animal with a snout that lives on a farm! It means that he is not very neat.

Connecting to Real Life

A final step is to **connect words to real life**. For example, think about the word *exciting*. Do you know what it means? Something exciting is a thing you can't wait to see or do. It makes you cheerful and thrilled! You truly know new words when you can use them to describe things in real life.

Example: Mia and her family took an exciting trip to a theme park.

As you learn more words, you also will see they can have **shades of meaning**. Related words can describe levels of an idea. Look at this example.

"Terry was glad about the surprise party," Marie said.

"Oh, I think he was happy," Frankie countered.

"No way!" Shaun piped up. "He was ecstatic!"

"Well," Marie concluded, "I know he was overjoyed about getting that new video game."

The words in this little story show different shades of a person being pleased.

Glad means slightly pleased.

Happy means delighted or definitely pleased.

Ecstatic means extremely pleased.

Overjoyed means feeling great joy.

Knowing the shades of meaning helps you understand what you read. It also helps you use the right word when you write.

Practice 1: Word Meaning

RF 3.c, 4.c, **L** 4–6 (DOK 2–3)

DIRECTIONS **Read the passage. Then answer the questions after it.**

Tornado!

A tornado is a creepy kind of storm. It is very dangerous and can cause much damage. It is a loud storm with very high winds. People say it sounds like a train coming. It often looks like a dark cloud with a cone shape at the bottom. If you ever see a cloud like that, look out! It could be a tornado.

There are some kinds of storms that may produce a tornado. When these come up, the weather service puts out a tornado watch. This means they will look for funnel clouds. These signal a tornado forming.

Other times, someone might see a tornado. It has already formed. Now the weather service puts out a tornado warning. If you hear a warning, a tornado may be near you. If this happens, then you must TAKE SHELTER. If you're outside, get inside your house. Go to the basement, if you have one. If there isn't a basement, go to a closet, a bathroom, or a hallway on the lowest level of your house. Stay away from windows. A tornado can destroy buildings and make everything fly around!

Tornadoes can be scary and harmful. But you can be safe during a tornado if you follow these steps.

Read this sentence from the first paragraph.

A tornado is a creepy kind of storm.

1 Which of these would be a better word to use than <u>creepy</u>?

A Eerie

B Peculiar

C Terrifying

D Bloodcurdling

Chapter 6

Read this sentence from the first paragraph.

It is very dangerous and can cause much damage.

2 Which word has three syllables?

A Very **B** Dangerous **C** Cause **D** Damage

3 Which word means the same as the word <u>produce</u> in paragraph 2?

A Make **B** Lessen **C** Stain **D** Arrive

4 In paragraph 2, <u>puts out</u> means —

A takes outside. **C** announces.

B sends away. **D** leaves.

5 The last paragraph says that tornadoes can be "scary and harmful." What do these words tell you about these storms?

____

____

Chapter 6 Summary

All the words you know are your **vocabulary**. To build your vocabulary, you need to learn new words. This helps you become a better reader and writer.

One of the best ways to figure out new words is to use **context clues**. This means looking at what is around a word to see what it means.

Syllables are chunks of sound. Reading one syllable at a time can help you read long words.

Some words have **multiple meanings**. They can mean different things, depending on how they are used.

Authors can paint pictures with words using **figurative language**.

When you **connect words to real life**, you see what new words truly mean. You also see they can have **shades of meaning**.

Chapter 6 Review

RF 3.c, 4.c, **L** 4–6 (DOK 2, 3)

DIRECTIONS **Read the poem, and then answer the questions.**

Ten-Layer Cake

I made a ten-layer cake
Out of twigs, berries, and dates.

I put some water in mud
And used it as glue
To keep the layers fixed
On my layered thing-a-ma-do.

I built it under the window in my yard
And sprinkled it with seeds and scraps,
To get the birds and squirrels to come
And fill up before their winter naps.

When I was finished,
My mom said, "Good job!"
As the animals came
To taste my thing-a-ma-bob.

The chipmunks gnawed at the dates.
The birds pecked at the seeds.
I even saw a little mouse as
The squirrels grabbed what they pleased.

But that night while I was asleep,
The rain came down hard and deep.

When I looked out my window,
My ten-layer cake was down …
Only the twigs remained
In a stack on the wet ground.

"Oh well," I thought,
As I got up and ready,
"I'll build another cake
While the sun is steady."

Chapter 6

1 Which word means the same as the word fixed in line 5?

A Correct **B** Broken **C** Flat **D** Off

Read line 7.

I built it under the window in my yard

2 What is the best definition for the word built?

A Put together from parts

B Made in a factory

C Became much louder

D Planned out

Read lines 19 and 20.

But that night while I was asleep
The rain came down hard and deep.

3 Which word has two syllables?

A Night **B** Asleep **C** Rain **D** Down

Read lines 23 and 24.

Only the twigs remained
In a small stack on the wet ground.

4 Which of these would be a better word to use than stack?

A Hoard **B** Mass **C** Load **D** Pile

5 In line 28, what does "While the sun is steady" mean? Use details from the poem to explain why you think it means that.

____

____

____

Read stanza 5.

The chipmunks gnawed at the dates.
The birds pecked at the seeds.
I saw a little mouse run away as
The squirrels grabbed what they pleased.

6 How does the author use figurative language in this stanza? What picture does the author paint in your mind?

____

____

____

____

____

Chapter 7
Spelling

This chapter covers DOK levels 1–3 and the following third grade strands and standards (for full standards, please see Appendix A):

Reading Foundational Skills: 3.a, b, d

Language: 4.b, c, d

SPELLING

You need to know how to spell words so you will know them when you read. You also must spell them correctly when you write. That way, people will know what you mean.

ROOTS, PREFIXES, AND SUFFIXES

The main part of a word is the **root**. New words can be made out of root words by adding beginnings (prefixes) and endings (suffixes). Words that have the same root word form word families.

For example, *clear* is a root. By adding prefixes and suffixes, you can make new words. Here are some of the words in this word family.

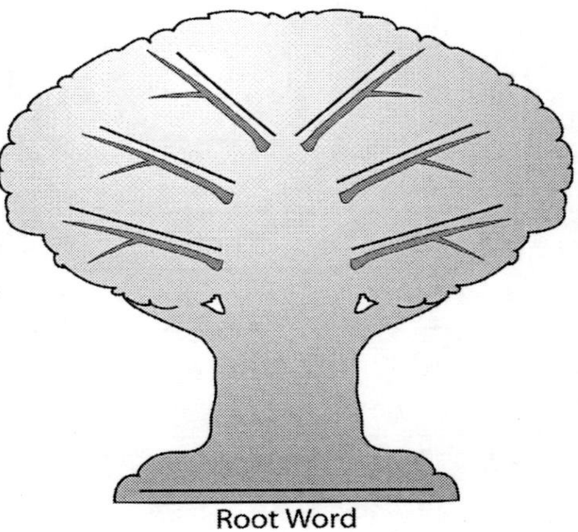

Examples:

un*clear*

*clear*ly

*clear*ed

Chapter 7

Here are a few more root words and their meanings:

Root	Meaning	Example
annu, anni	year	*annu*al, *anni*versary
aqua	water	*aqua*rium
aud	to hear	*aud*ible
bio	life	*bio*logy
deca	ten	*deca*de
multi	many	*multi*ply
path	feeling	*path*etic, sym*path*ize
phon	sound	tele*phon*e

Root words also help you figure out new words. For example, you know what the word *cave* means. It is a hollow or a passage in a mountain or in the earth. Knowing the word *cave* gives you clues to other words. What does *cavity* mean? It has the same root. A cavity is a hole, like in a tooth. How about the word *excavate*? It has the same root too. It means to dig or scoop out. Now you see how to use root words to figure out new words.

A **prefix** is one or more letters that go at the start of a word.

Prefix	Meaning	Example
bi-	two or twice	*bi*lingual, *bi*cycle
dis-	to take away, the opposite of	*dis*respect
mis-	wrong or badly	*mis*behave, *mis*inform
re-	again	*re*view, *re*read, *re*play
tri-	three	*tri*plets
im-, in-, un-	not	*im*possible, *in*formal, *un*able

When a prefix is added to a root word, the spelling of the root word does not change.

dis + like = dislike

un + happy = unhappy

mis + understand = misunderstand

A **suffix** is one or more letters that go at the end of a word.

Suffix	Meaning	Example
-er	someone who does something	runn*er*, bak*er*, garden*er*
-ful	full of	cheer*ful,* plenti*ful*, fright*ful*
-less	without	fear*less*, hope*less*
-ly	like, in the manner of	quiet*ly*, easi*ly*
-ment	a state of being	entertain*ment*, amaze*ment*, content*ment*
-ous	full of or having	spaci*ous*, graci*ous*

When a **suffix** is added to a root word, the spelling of that word might change.

1 If the suffix starts with a vowel (*a*, *e*, *i*, *o*, *u*) and is added to a word ending in a silent *e*, then drop the silent *e*.

please + ing = pleasing

like + able = likable

2 If the suffix starts with a consonant and is added to a word that ends in a silent *e*, then the *e* stays.

love + ly = lovely

Practice 1: Roots, Prefixes, and Suffixes

RF 3.a, b, **L** 4.b (DOK 1–2)

DIRECTIONS **Read the questions, and then choose the right answers.**

1 What is the root in the word review?

A rev **B** vie **C** view **D** ew

2 Which of the following words has a prefix that means to "take away"?

A Misguided **B** Disable **C** Repeat **D** Undo

3 If you add the suffix *-ous* to the root joy, the new word, joyous, means —

A a maker of joy.

B an act of joy.

C without joy.

D full of joy.

4 You see the word circumference in your math book. Which word can most likely help you figure out what it means?

A Circle **B** Fence **C** Refer **D** Corner

5 Which suffix would you add to the word home to make it mean "without a home"?

A -ful **B** -ly **C** -less **D** -er

6 Based on what you know about roots and suffixes, what does the word formulate mean? Explain your answer.

Odd Spellings

You will need to learn some words by memory. This is because they have **irregular spellings**. *Irregular* means odd or unusual. English words come from many other languages. Some words use the spelling rules of the language they came from. Here are some examples.

Word	How you say it	Why
enough	ee-**nuf**	In some words, *gh* sounds like *f*. Most of these come from German. Other examples are *tough* and *laughter*.
should	sh*uh*d	The *l* is silent, like it is in *walk* and *calf*. Many of these words come from Old Norse.

The *i* before *e* Rule

You might already know the famous ***i* before *e* rule**. It goes like this: "Put *i* before *e*, except after *c*, or when sounded like *a* as in *neighbor* and *weigh*." It's a good rule most of the time. Take a look at these words.

siege, receipt, brief, deceive, grieve, believe, ceiling

However, there are plenty of words that do not follow this rule, like *protein, scientist, beige, society, heist, glacier,* and *ancient.* You will simply need to learn these words one by one. Some words are just weird. Hey, there's another one: *weird.*

THE *Y* TO *I* RULE

When a word ends in *y*, you usually **change the *y* to *i*** when you add a suffix.

happy + ness = happiness

scurry + ed = scurried

But don't change the *y* to *i* if you are adding the suffix *ing.*

try + ing = trying

carry + ing = carrying

Here is another exception. If the word has a vowel before the *y*, then keep the *y* before adding a suffix.

destroy + er = destroyer

play + ed = played

CONSONANT DOUBLING

Consonant doubling is just what it says. When you add certain suffixes to words, you might have to add another consonant. Here is a way to know when to double a consonant. Ask yourself three questions:

1 Does the word have one syllable?

2 Does the word have one vowel?

3 Does the word have one consonant at the end?

If you answer "yes" to ALL of these questions, then double the consonant. If you answer "no" to any of them, do not double it. Look at the examples on the next page.

hop

one syllable? YES

one vowel? YES

one consonant at end? YES

Change it!

hop + ed = hopped

sing

one syllable? YES

one vowel? YES

one consonant at end? NO

Don't change it!

sing + ing = singing

Homophones

Homophones are words that sound alike but are spelled differently. They do not really follow a specific rule. They are just words that you need to learn. Once you learn the difference between the words, you can know the spelling. Here are some common homophones:

Some Common Homophones				
allowed aloud	cell sell	hear here	plane plain	they're there their
band banned	for four	knot not	real reel	to too two
bear bare	guest guessed	one won	right write	weather whether

There are many more of these words. Do your best to learn them so you don't confuse them.

Frequently Misspelled Words				
about	children	friend	house	money
always	didn't	girl	I'd	school
around	don't	give	I'm	started
because	every	gone	know	third
become	family	head	learn	while

SPELLING RESOURCES

Some words do not follow rules. They have to be learned and remembered. One way to learn tricky words is to keep a journal. If you always misspell certain words, write them out in a notebook or on a 3 × 5 card. Then you can review them and learn them.

Also, instead of guessing at the spelling of a word, use a spelling resource. This could be a **dictionary**, a **thesaurus**, or a **glossary**. A dictionary has words in ABC order. Many words start with the same letters. A dictionary will also show you how to pronounce a word. Here is a sample dictionary entry.

daughter daw-ter *noun*
(entry) (pronunciation) (part of speech)

1. the female child of parents.
(definition)

They have a daughter and a son.
(sample sentence)

Many resources are online as well. For instance, you can use an online dictionary to look up words. Also, when you write, be sure to use the spell checker on your computer.

Practice 2: Spelling

RF 3.d, **L** 2.e, f, g (DOK 1)

DIRECTIONS **Read and then answer the questions.**

1 In this sentence, which underlined word is not spelled correctly?

There are three horsees grazing in the fields.

A three **B** horsees **C** grazing **D** fields

2 Which underlined word is not spelled correctly?

Those gooses can bite, so be careful.

A gooses **B** bite **C** so **D** careful

kind•ness kynd-nis *noun*

1. the state of being kind

I will never forget your kindness.

3 Which is the correct spelling of the entry?

A kind-ness **B** kynd-nis **C** kindness **D** kyndness

scream *verb*

1. to cry out

synonyms: yell, holler, squeal

antonyms: be silent, whisper

4 What is the definition of the word?

A yell **B** be silent **C** to cry out **D** verb

5 Which is an antonym for the word?

A yell **B** holler **C** squeal **D** whisper

6 Which underlined word is not spelled correctly?

My principal walkd down the hall.

A principal **B** walkd **C** down **D** hall

7 Which is the correct spelling of the plural form of party?

A partys **B** partes **C** partyes **D** parties

8 Which word is not spelled correctly?

A earring **B** yearning **C** noticable **D** singing

CHAPTER 7 SUMMARY

There are many **spelling** rules. Keep in mind that many rules may have exceptions!

A **root** is the main part of a word. Other parts can be added to it. Knowing roots and their **word families** helps you figure out new words.

When a **prefix** is added to a root word, the spelling of the root word does not change.

When a **suffix** is added to a root word, the spelling of that word might change.

Put ***i* before *e***, except after *c*, or when sounded like *a* as in *neighbor* and *weigh*.

When a word ends in *y*, you usually **change the *y* to *i*** when you add a suffix (unless it has a vowel before the *y*, then don't change it).

Consonant doubling is just what it says: when you add certain suffixes to words, you might have to double the consonant (if the word has one syllable, one vowel, and one consonant at the end).

Homophones are words that sound alike but are spelled differently.

You can look up words in a **dictionary**, a **thesaurus**, or a **glossary**.

Chapter 7 Review

RF 3.a, b, d, **L** 4.b, c, d (DOK 1–3)

DIRECTIONS **Read the passage. It contains mistakes. Then answer the questions.**

Wishing There Was Another Way

I sitted in the waiting room of the doctor's office. It was time for my yearly flu shot. There were about a dozen other kids in there. No one was smileing and most of them looked really bored.

As I waited, I could feel my heart beating quickly. I had butterflies in my stomach. My skin felt cold but sweaty. I looked up at the ceiling and tried to imagine blew sky. It didn't work. I mostly noticed some stains on the ceiling, which made me think the rain had leaked in sometime in the past.

I picked up a magazine, but I was unable to read. All I did was flip through the pages. I kept looking at the clock, wishing that time would go by quickly so I could get this over with. Time went as slowly as it did in school when it was nice outside and everone waited for the last bell.

Read this sentence from paragraph 1.

I sitted in the waiting room of the doctor's office.

1 Which word should be changed, and why? How would you correct it?

____

____

Read this sentence from paragraph 1.

No one was smileing and most of them looked really bored.

2 Which word is not spelled correctly?

A waiting **B** yearly **C** smileing **D** really

Read this sentence from paragraph 2.

I had <u>butterflies</u> in my stomach.

3 What is the correct way to spell the underlined word?

A butterflys **C** buterflies

B butterflyes **D** correct as is

Read this sentence from paragraph 2.

I looked up at the ceiling and tried to imagine blew sky.

4 Which word is not spelled correctly?

A looked **B** ceiling **C** tried **D** blew

Read this sentence from paragraph 2.

I mostly noticed some stains on the ceiling, which made me think the rain had leaked in sometime in the past.

Now read this dictionary entry for the word <u>leak</u>.

leak *noun*
1. a crack or gap where something gets in or out
2. telling of a secret, like to the media
leak *verb*
1. to let a liquid, gas, or light escape
2. to become known without meaning to (*The news leaked out.*)

5 Which definition is correct for how the word is used in the sentence?

A Noun 1

B Noun 2

C Verb 1

D Verb 2

Read this sentence from paragraph 3.

I picked up a magazine, but I was unable to read.

6 You may know that the word *able* means "to have the power or skill to do something." So, adding the prefix *un-* makes the word unable mean —

A "not interested in doing something."

B "curious about doing something."

C "too careful to do something."

D "talented at something."

Read this sentence from paragraph 3.

I kept looking at the clock, wishing that time would go by faster, so I could get it over with.

7 What part is the suffix in the word looking?

A look

B oki

C king

D ing

Read this sentence from paragraph 3.

Time went as slowly as it did in school when it was nice outside and everone *waited for the last bell.*

8 Which is the correct spelling of the underlined word?

A evryone

B everione

C everyone

D Correct as is

Chapter 8
Parts of Speech

This chapter covers DOK levels 1–3 and the following third grade strands and standards (for full standards, please see Appendix A):

Writing: 1.c, 2.c, 3.c

Language: 1.a–i

Parts of Speech

Words are the building blocks we use to create our messages. Sentences are made up of words. Every word has a role to play.

The way each word works in a sentence explains its part of speech. There are eight **parts of speech**. In this chapter, we will look at each of the eight parts of speech.
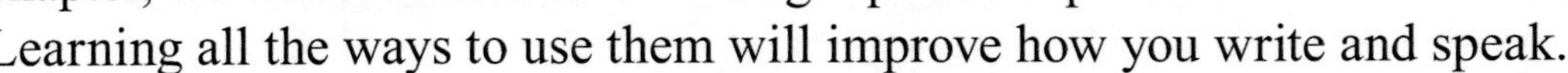
Learning all the ways to use them will improve how you write and speak.

Nouns

A **noun** is a word that names a person, place, thing, or idea. Look at the following sentence.

The boy went to school on the bus.

In this sentence, *boy*, *school*, and *bus* are all nouns. A boy is a person. School is a place and thing. A bus is also a thing.

Singular nouns name just one of something. Plural nouns mean more than one. Most of the time, you just add an *s* or *es* to make a noun plural. Look at these examples.

masks

songs

boxes

potatoes

Some plural nouns are **irregular**. To make them plural, you have to change the spelling. Some words don't change at all. Look at these words.

men (more than one man)

oxen (more than one ox)

fungi (more than one fungus)

sheep (stays the same for singular and plural)

There is not a specific rule for words like these. You just have to learn them.

An **abstract noun** names an idea, feeling, quality, or concept. Abstract nouns are things that you are not able to touch or see, such as *courage*. You can see someone being brave, but courage itself is an idea. Look at these examples.

Johnny felt anger toward the bully on the playground.

The abstract noun is *anger*. It is an emotion.

A good education can help you succeed in the future.

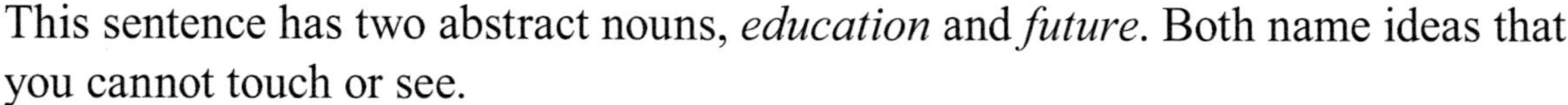

This sentence has two abstract nouns, *education* and *future*. Both name ideas that you cannot touch or see.

Here are some abstract nouns that you may often see.

Abstract Nouns			
anger	education	joy	sadness
calm	faith	peace	trust
courage	humor	sleep	worry

Pronouns

A **pronoun** is a word used in the place of one or more nouns.

Ted says <u>he</u> likes math better than history.

In this sentence, *he* is a pronoun. It takes the place of the noun *Ted*.

The pronoun must agree in number (one or more) and gender (male or female) with what it replaces. This is called **pronoun-antecedent agreement**. An antecedent (an-t*uh*-seed-*uh*nt) is whatever word the pronoun replaces. So, in the sentence above, *Ted* is the antecedent. Ted is a boy, and he is just one person. So, the pronoun *he* is correct. Now, look at this example.

Kira and Sallie are studying together because they want to do well on the science test.

Kira and Sallie are two people. This means both their names can be replaced with the plural pronoun *they*. The plural pronouns have no gender.

A **possessive pronoun** shows that something belongs to a person. Look at these examples.

Amanda left her lunch box at school.

The possessive pronoun *her* shows that *Amanda* owns the lunch box.

My mom and dad just had their wedding anniversary.

The possessive pronoun *their* shows that the anniversary is *mom* and *dad*'s.

A **personal pronoun** refers to a specific person, place, or thing. Look at these examples.

People think Randy is funny because he tells good jokes.

The personal pronoun *he* takes the place of the noun *Randy*.

Emily and David saw the movie the weekend it came out.

The personal pronoun *it* takes the place of the noun *movie*.

Here is a list of personal pronouns that you should know.

Personal Pronouns		
	Singular	**Plural**
First Person	I, me, my, mine	we, us, our, ours
Second Person	you, your, yours	you, your, yours
Third Person	he, him, his, she, her, hers, it, its	they, them, their, theirs

Practice 1: Nouns and Pronouns

L 1.a–c, f (DOK 1, 3)

DIRECTIONS **Read the passage. It contains mistakes. Then answer the questions.**

Baseball Uniforms

(1) A baseball player wears a uniform. (2) This shows which team he plays for. (3) Each uniform has the team's name on it. (4) The colors of the uniforms make a team easy to recognize, which helps fans cheer and get in the spirit of the game!

(5) The player's last name goes on the back of the shirt. (6) Each player has a number, and _____ goes on the back of the shirt too. (7) Some uniforms have a small number on the front as well.

(8) Baseball players also wear pants, socks, and a cap. (9) Some have a glove. (10) They wear special shoes called spikes. (11) These shoes have little pins on the bottom. (12) These help players run better.

(13) Each team has certain colors. (14) Players wear white when they play in his own city. (15) They wear a dark color when they play in other citys.

Read sentence 4.

The colors of the uniforms make a team easy to recognize, which helps fans cheer and get in the spirit of the game!

1 Which noun in this sentence is an abstract noun? What makes it abstract?

____

____

____

____

Read sentence 6.

Each player has a number, and ____ goes on the back of the shirt too.

2 What is the correct pronoun to put in the blank space?

A he **B** it **C** she **D** they

Read sentence 14.

Players wear white when they play in <u>his</u> own city.

3 What is the correct way to write the underlined pronoun?

A their **B** its **C** her **D** Correct as is

Read sentence 15.

They wear a dark color when hey play in other <u>citys</u>.

4 What is the correct way to write the underlined noun?

A cittys **B** citis **C** cities **D** Correct as is

VERBS

A **verb** is a word used to express action or state of being.

Daniel and Malik <u>skate</u> down the block.

In this sentence, *skate* is a word that expresses action.

I <u>am</u> really tired.

In this sentence, the verb is *am*. It is what is called a "state of being" verb. These verbs are forms of the verb *to be*. They include *is*, *are*, *was*, *were*, *be*, *being*, *been*.

Verb tense identifies when an action takes place. The three basic verb tenses are **past**, **present**, and **future**.

Chapter 8

Let's look at some verbs and how they change tenses.

Basic Verb Tenses

Past	Present	Future
I ate	I eat	I will eat
I sat	I sit	I will sit
I slept	I sleep	I will sleep
I stopped	I stop	I will stop
I wrote	I write	I will write

Like some nouns, some verbs are **irregular**. That means they change spelling when they change tenses. Look at the verbs in the last table. Here are some other examples.

sing → *sang*
take → *took*
bring → *brought*

In every sentence, the verb must agree with the subject. The subject is what the sentence is about. If the subject is singular, it needs a singular verb. If the subject is plural, it needs a plural verb. This is called **subject-verb agreement**.

Singular subject:

Mia drives her sister to school.

Austin is the capital of Texas.

Plural subject:

Cows eat hay.

Will and Caleb play baseball on the same team.

Adjectives and Adverbs

An **adjective** is a word that describes or adds details to a noun or pronoun. An adjective tells what kind, which one, how much, or how many. The most common adjectives are *a, an*, and *the*. These are called **articles**. But there are many others that add vivid description. Let's take a look at some adjectives.

The huge, hairy beast roared, scaring the villagers away.

Huge and *hairy* are adjectives in this sentence. They tell what kind of beast.

We saw fourteen flamingos at the zoo.

Fourteen is an adjective that tells how many flamingos.

An **adverb** is another type of word that describes or adds details. It can modify a verb, an adjective, or another adverb. Adverbs add details in many ways. They can tell the following:

- **time** (when?)
- **place** (where?)
- **manner** (how?)
- **degree** (how much? to what extent?)

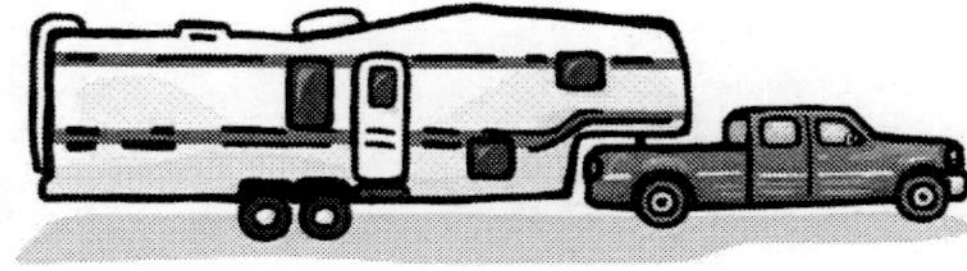

Now, let's look at some adverbs.

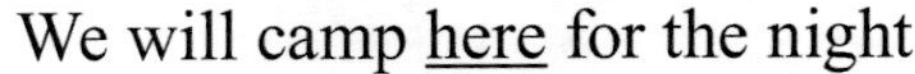

We will camp here for the night.

Here is an adverb. It tells where we will camp for the night.

The boy ran quickly to get out of the rain.

Quickly is an adverb. It tells how the boy ran.

Comparatives and Superlatives

Comparative adjectives show how two objects are alike or not alike. We usually add the suffix *-er* to the end of the adjective to show this comparison. **Superlative adjectives** compare more than two objects. We use the suffix *-est* to show this comparison.

If you wanted to compare two runners in a race, you might say that one is faster than the other. *Faster* is a comparative adjective. If you wanted to compare the winner of the race to all of the runners, you might say the winner of the race was the fastest. *Fastest* is a superlative adjective because it is used to compare more than two objects.

Comparative and Superlative Adjectives		
Adjective	**Comparative**	**Superlative**
rich	richer	richest
short	shorter	shortest
fast	faster	fastest
slow	slower	slowest
small	smaller	smallest
big	bigger	biggest

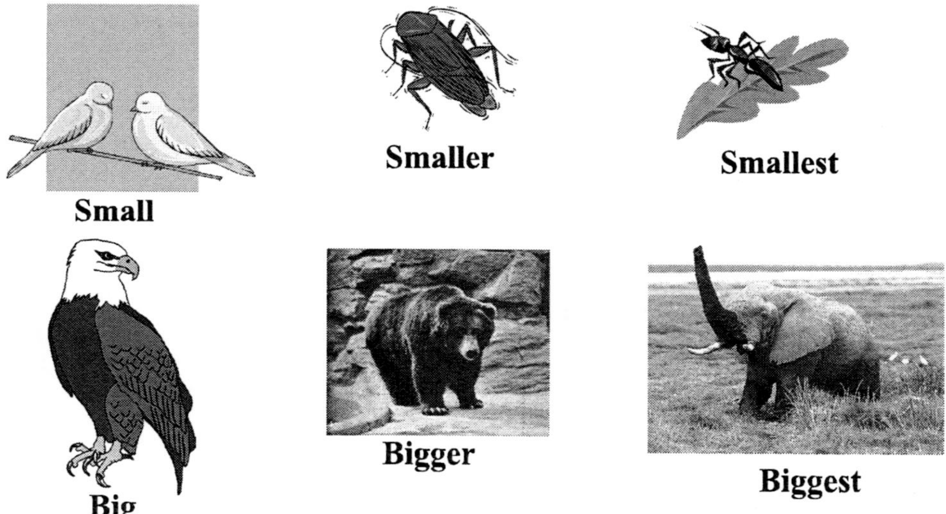

Just like adjectives, there are **comparative and superlative adverbs**. Some of these adverbs use the same suffixes *-er* and *-est*. Adverbs that end in the suffix *-ly* are not changed. Instead we add *more* or *most* in front of the adverb when comparing.

Comparative and Superlative Adverbs		
Adverb	**Comparative**	**Superlative**
quietly	more quietly	most quietly
seriously	more seriously	most seriously

Practice 2: Verbs, Adjectives, and Adverbs

L 1.d, e, g (DOK 1–3)

DIRECTIONS **Read the passage. It contains mistakes. Then answer the questions that follow.**

Jewel Makers of the Sea

(1) It was 4,500 years ago that people finded pearls. (2) The Chinese discovered them in oysters. (3) Oysters is animals that live in shells in the ocean. (4) People eat oysters, but they probably never expected this gift from the little creatures.

(5) There is a special coating on the inside of an oyster shell. (6) It is called mother-of-pearl. (7) It is shiny and smooth. (8) It keeps the oyster safe and comfortable. (9) At times, a grain of sand can get into the shell. (10) If it gets caught inside, this can hurt the soft little oyster. (11) So the oyster covers the grain of sand with lots of layers of mother-of-pearl. (12) It protects itself so it doesn't get scratched by the sand.

(13) The oyster works hard to make the grain soft and smooth and silky. (14) Over time, that grain of sand became a pearl. (15) A pearl is round, smooth, and shiny. (16) It looks like a little white marble. (17) Really, it is just a grain of sand covered in many layers of mother-of-pearl.

(18) It takes an oyster about two to four years to careful make a good-sized pearl. (19) Not all oyster shells have pearls in them. (20) So pearls are rare. (21) People use pearls to make jewelry. (22) You may have seen pearl earrings, necklaces, or bracelets. (23) People like pearls because they are pretty jewels. (24) To the oysters, pearls are just a problem to get rid of!

Read sentence 1.

It was 4,500 years ago that people <u>finded</u> pearls.

1 What is the correct way to write the underlined verb in this sentence?

A find

B found

C founded

D Correct as is

Read sentence 3.

Oysters is animals that live in shells in the ocean.

2 What is the correct way to write the underlined verb?

A are **B** was **C** being **D** Correct as is

Read sentence 10.

If it gets caught inside, this can hurt the soft little oyster.

3 What is the correct way to write the underlined verb?

A catch **B** catched **C** caughted **D** Correct as is

Read sentence 11.

So the oyster covers the grain of sand with lots of layers of mother-of-pearl.

4 What is the best adjective to use in place of the underlined words?

____

____

Read sentence 14.

Over time, that grain of sand became a pearl.

5 What is the correct way to write the underlined verb?

A become **C** becoming

B becomes **D** Correct as is

Read sentence 18.

It takes an oyster about two to four years to careful make a good-sized pearl.

6 What is the correct way to write the underlined adverb?

A carely **B** carefuly **C** carefully **D** Correct as is

Prepositions

A **preposition** is a word used to show a relationship. Some tell directions (*on*, *in*, *under*, *around*). Some help show time (*after*, *until*, *while*). Others show contrast (*but*, *although*). There are many prepositions. Learn to use the right one to say what you mean. Here are some examples.

The cat ran under the table.

My homework is in my backpack.

The crying boy ran behind his older brother.

She baked the cookies after mixing in the chocolate chips.

Conjunctions

A **conjunction** is a word used to join words or groups of words. You can remember them by thinking of the word **FANBOYS**.

For
And
Nor
But
Or
Yet
So

Examples:

Bobbie and Allie walk to school together.

Shelly likes peanut butter, but she doesn't like jelly.

We could not see if Rafael or Taylor caught the ball.

There are different kinds of conjunctions. You will read more about these in the next section. They play an important role in sentences.

Transitions

Transitions are words and phrases that link ideas. You just read about conjunctions and prepositions. Some of these can be used as transition words. They can help link ideas in sentences.

Examples:

Gena ate her sandwich while Jimmy watched TV.

After they practiced, they ate a big lunch.

First, I looked both ways, and then I crossed the street.

Practice 3: Prepositions, Transitions, and Conjunctions

W 1.c, 2.c, 3.c, L 1.h (DOK 1–3)

DIRECTIONS **Read the passage. It contains mistakes. Then answer the questions.**

The American Flag

(1) There are several facts you might not know about the American flag. (2) Our flag is sometimes called the Stars and Stripes or Old Glory. (3) It is full of symbols.

(4) For example, it has thirteen stripes or fifty stars. (5) The thirteen stripes stand for the first thirteen colonies. (6) The fifty stars stand for the fifty states on the United States.

(7) Even the colors stand for something important. (8) The red stands for bravery. (9) The white stands for loyalty. (10) That means being true to your country. (11) The color blue stands for justice or being fair.

(12) Our flag reminds Americans of the brave people who fought for our country. (13) _____ you look at the flag, think about what it stands for.

Read sentence 4.

For example, it has thirteen stripes or fifty stars.

1 What is the best way to write the underlined conjunction?

A and **B** until **C** above **D** Correct as is

Read sentence 6.

The fifty stars stand for the fifty states on the United States.

2 What is the best way to write the underlined preposition?

A in
B until
C above
D Correct as is

Read sentence 7.

Even the colors stand for something important.

3 What is the best way to write the underlined transition?
A Yet **B** Although **C** So **D** Correct as is

Read sentence 13.

_______ *you look at the flag, think about what it stands for.*

4 What is the best transition to write in the blank?

____

____

Working with Sentences

A **sentence** is a group of words. These words work together to tell a complete thought.

Here are two things to know about sentences:

- A sentence must have a subject and a verb.
- A sentence is also called an *independent clause*.

Simple Sentences

A **simple sentence** has a subject and a verb. It is one independent clause. An independent clause is a sentence that can stand on its own.

Here are some examples of simple sentences. The subject in each sentence is underlined. The verb is in italics (*slanted type*).

Examples:

Russ *bought* a chocolate ice cream cone.

D'Nae *raked* leaves in the yard.

Toby and Rhea *like* the same kinds of songs.

Chapter 8

Compound Sentences

A **compound sentence** joins two sentences with a comma and a **conjunction**. These conjunctions can be used to join two sentences:

for, and, nor, but, or, yet, so

When joining two sentences, always put a comma before the conjunction. Here are some examples of compound sentences. The conjunctions are underlined.

Examples:

I want to play soccer, but I also want to swim.

Do you want pizza for dinner, or do you want burgers for dinner?

He sings really well, and he can dance too.

Complex Sentences

A **complex sentence** has one independent clause. It also has at least one dependent clause. A dependent clause cannot stand on its own. It is not a complete sentence. Let's look at an example.

When you go in the kitchen, you will find some cookies.

In this sentence, the second part is an independent clause. It expresses a complete thought, and it could stand alone. You will find some cookies.

The first part of the sentence is a dependent clause. It does not express a complete thought. "When you go in the kitchen" cannot stand alone.

Often a **conjunction** will join these clauses. Look at this example.

Many middle school students enjoy chatting with friends while eating lunch.

The first part is the independent clause. "Many middle school students enjoy chatting with friends" can stand alone.

The underlined word is the subordinating conjunction. It starts the dependent clause, "while eating lunch." It can't stand alone.

Here are some other conjunctions:

after, as, although, because, before, even if, just as, since, so that, when, where

Practice 4: Working with Sentences

L 1.i (DOK 1–3)

DIRECTIONS **Read the passage. Then answer the questions after it.**

What's Your Favorite Cookie?

1 I have never met a person who does not like cookies. Not all people like the same type. But most of us like some kind of cookies. One of the most popular is the chocolate chip cookie. It's easy to see why. What's more comforting than a warm, gooey chocolate chip cookie?

2 The chocolate chip cookie had quite a start. Its history is like a legend. No one is quite sure how the chocolate chip cookie came about. Here's the story that most people know. In 1934, a lady named Ruth Wakefield owned the Toll House Inn. People came to stay there overnight. She loved making cookies for her) uests. It made the inn smell good. It was a nice treat.

3 One day, she ran out of baker's chocolate. She needed it for the chocolate cookies she was making. She did not have time to buy any. She had all the other ingredients: flour, eggs, butter, sugar, and chopped nuts. So, she just broke up pieces of Nestlé semisweet chocolate and mixed them in. But the chocolate did not melt into the dough like she wanted. The pieces stayed in their solid form, although they melted a little bit.

4 Everyone loved the new cookies. Mrs. Wakefield sold the recipe to Nestlé. In return, the people at Nestlé gave her chocolate chips to make more cookies. In fact, they gave her a lifetime supply! Now every bag of Nestlé chocolate chips has Mrs. Wakefield's original recipe on it.

5 That's the story that has been passed down. It may or may not be completely true. No matter what, we're all glad chocolate chip cookies were created!

Read these sentences from paragraph 2.

It made the inn smell good. It was a nice treat.

1 What is the best way to combine these sentences?

____

____

Chapter 8

Read this sentence from paragraph 3.

One day, she ran out of baker's chocolate.

2 What kind of sentence is this?

A Simple

B Compound

C Complex

D It is not a sentence.

Read this sentence from paragraph 3.

The pieces stayed in their solid form, although they melted a little bit.

3 Which word is the conjunction?

A stayed

B in

C although

D bit

Read this sentence from paragraph 5.

No matter what, we're all glad chocolate chip cookies were created!

4 Which part of this sentence is an independent clause?

A The first part

B The second part

C Both parts

D Neither part

Chapter 8 Summary

A **noun** is a word that names a person, place, thing, or idea.

A **pronoun** is a word used in the place of one or more nouns.

A **verb** is a word used to express action or state of being.

An **adverb** is a word used to describe or add details to a verb, an adjective, or another adverb.

An **adjective** is a word used to describe or add details to a noun or pronoun.

A **preposition** is a word used to show the relationship of a noun or a pronoun to another word.

Transitions help link ideas in a sentence.

A **conjunction** is a word used to join words or groups of words.

A **simple sentence** is one independent clause. A **compound sentence** has two independent clauses.

A **complex sentence** has one independent clause.

A comma plus a **coordinating conjunction** can join the two clauses.

Chapter 8 Review

W 1.c, 2.c, 3.c L 1.a–i (DOK 1–3)

DIRECTIONS **Read the passage. It contains mistakes. Then answer the questions.**

The Golden Spike

1 In the early 1800s, travel was slow. Some people used the stagecoach. It was expensive and taked a long time. There were bandits and robbers along the way. Others traveled by covered wagon. It was scary. Sometimes they ran out of supplys. As a result, there was just no easy way to go from the East to California.

Early Railroad Workers

2 The railroad companies had an idea. They said they would build tracks across America. It would make travel fastest. It would also be safer. They would call it the Transcontinental Railroad. It would go all the way across the continent. Congress gave land for the tracks. Work start on the tracks in 1862.

3 In all, progress was slow due to the Civil War. When the war ended, more men could work about the railroad. This is how the tracks were laid faster. They would soon meet in the middle. The east and west sides came closer together. New towns sprang up along the tracks. The workers laid tracks in hard winters and across very hot desert. They finished the railroad.

4 On May 10, 1869, the two sides of the tracks met at Promontory Summit, Utah. A golden spike was used to nail in the last piece of track. It was made of gold because this was a big event. The spike is a symbol of the nation being joined by the new railroad.

Read this sentence from paragraph 1.

It was expensive and taked a long time.

1 What is the correct way to write the underlined verb in this sentence?

A take **B** took **C** taking **D** Correct as is

Read this sentence from paragraph 1.

It was scary.

2 In this sentence, the pronoun "It" refers to what?

____

____

Read this sentence from paragraph 1.

Sometimes they ran out of supplys.

3 What is the correct way to write the underlined noun?

A supplyes

B supplies

C supplise

D Correct as is

Read these sentences from paragraph 2.

The railroad companies had an idea. They said they would build tracks across America.

4 Which noun in these sentences is an abstract noun? What makes it abstract?

____

____

Read this sentence from paragraph 2.

It would make travel fastest.

5 What is the correct way to write the underlined adjective?

A fast

B faster

C fasterest

D Correct as is

Chapter 8

Read this sentence from paragraph 2.

Work start on the tracks in 1862.

6 What is the correct way to write the past tense of the underlined verb?

____

Read this sentence from paragraph 3.

In all, progress was slow due to the Civil War.

7 What is the best way to write the underlined transition?

A At first
B Suddenly
C And
D Correct as is

Read this sentence from paragraph 3.

When the war ended, more men could work about the railroad.

8 What is the best way to write the underlined preposition?

A of
B on
C below
D Correct as is

Read these sentences from paragraph 3.

The workers laid tracks in hard winters and across very hot desert. They finished the railroad.

9 What is the best way to combine these sentences?

____

____

____

Read this sentence from paragraph 4.

On May 10, 1869, the two sides of the tracks met at Promontory Summit, Utah.

10 What kind of sentence is this?

A Simple

B Compound

C Complex

D It is not a sentence.

DIRECTIONS **Read this passage. Underline all of the conjunctions in it.**

First Camping Trip

This summer, I went on my first camping trip. It was with a group from the community center. Everyone was restless while we waited for the van to pick us up. Our backpacks, tents, and sleeping bags were all over the sidewalk. We spent the weeks looking for and buying all the equipment we would need. We waited a while, so we were a little upset that the van arrived late. We all wanted to get going, but we had to load the gear on board. When that was done, we took off—better late than never. At least we were on our way, although we would get there late. Our parents waved goodbye as we drove off. Finally, we arrived at camp. It was exciting because we all knew it would be a great week!

Chapter 9
Conventions and Usage

This chapter covers DOK levels 1–3 and the following third grade strands and standards (for full standards, please see Appendix A):

Language: 2.a–d, 3.a, b

There are some important rules about using language. These rules help readers to understand text. When you write, you need to keep them in mind. When you use them well, people will know what you mean.

Conventions

Conventions are rules in language. This includes knowing which words to capitalize. It also includes how to use punctuation marks. Let's look at some of these rules.

Capitalization

Some words use **capitalization**. It is important to know when to capitalize words. You may ask, "How do I know which words to capitalize?" There are rules to help you figure it out.

Certain words are always capitalized. You probably know these rules already.

What to Capitalize	Examples
The word *I*	She told me I looked nice.
The first word in a sentence	He ran faster than ever before.
Names of days and months	Monday, January
Proper names	Macy, Keith, Aunt Linda, Mr. Kincaid
Proper places	Cambodia, Louisiana, Breckinridge Elementary School
Titles of books, songs, magazines, poems, and so on	*Freckle Juice*, "Jack and the Beanstalk"

Capital Letters in Titles

Look at the examples of **capital letters in titles** in the table above. The main words are capitalized. For the title of a book, story, song, poem, play, and so on, here are the rules:

1 Capitalize the first and last words.

2 Also capitalize all nouns, pronouns, verbs, adjectives, and adverbs.

3 Other words are not capitalized, unless one of them comes at the start of the title. The words not capitalized are articles (a, an, the), prepositions (words like *after*, *around*, *in*, *on*, *under*, *while*), and conjunctions (*for*, *and*, *nor*, *but*, *or*, *yet*, *so*).

Look at these examples. The articles, prepositions, and conjunctions are underlined. The rest of the words all need to start with capital letters. Look at the third example. The preposition *on* is capitalized. That's because it comes last in the title.

Examples:

The True Story of the Three Little Pigs

Where the Mountain Meets the Moon

"My Neighbor Is a Monster, Pass It On"

Direct Quotations

Writing exactly what someone says is called a **direct quotation**. Always capitalize the first word. Put quotation marks around the quoted words. Finally, use commas to separate the quotation from the rest of the sentence.

Examples:

Mr. White said, "Be here next Saturday at 9:00 a.m."

"Police chased the man all the way to Main Street," said the reporter.

Sometimes a sentence in a quotation is interrupted by words such as *he said.* In this case, do not use a capital letter to begin the second part of the quotation.

Examples:

"Chrissy," said Jill, "can you go with me?"

"After all that work," Brock asked, "why did you quit?"

Practice 1: Capitalization

L 2.a (DOK 1–2)

DIRECTIONS **Read the passage. It contains mistakes. Then answer each question.**

Rise and Shine

When I woke up, my cat skittles was curled up next to me, her furry body snuggled against my legs. Yesterday, she sat on my lap as we watched the movie *how to train your dragon*. It seemed we were never apart when I was home.

We got out of bed. Skittles followed me to the bathroom. We washed together. She licked her paws and belly, and I washed my face and brushed my teeth. Then, we went to the kitchen to eat our breakfasts.

After we ate, we got dressed. I put on her favorite red collar. She played with the laces on my shoes as I put on clothes for school. Finally, I said, "goodbye. You be a good girl today," and petted her head. I went out to catch the bus to school. I looked back. My cat was at the window, looking back at me.

Read the first sentence.

When I woke up, my cat skittles was curled up next to me, her furry body snuggled against my legs.

1 Which word in this sentence needs to be capitalized?

A cat **B** skittles **C** me **D** snuggled

2 What is the correct way to write the second sentence?

A Yesterday, she sat on my lap as we watched the movie *How to Train Your Dragon.*

B Yesterday, she sat on my lap as we watched the movie *How To Train Your Dragon.*

C Yesterday, she sat on my lap as we watched the movie *How to train your dragon.*

D Yesterday, she sat on my lap as we watched the movie *How to train your Dragon.*

3 What is the correct way to write this sentence from the third paragraph?

A Finally, I said, "goodbye. you be a good girl today," and petted her head.

B Finally, I said, "Goodbye. You be a good girl today," And petted her head.

C Finally, I said, "Goodbye. You be a good girl today," and petted her head.

D Finally, I said, "Goodbye. You Be a Good Girl Today," and petted her head.

Punctuation

Punctuation includes periods, commas, and other marks that help you know how to read a sentence. In chapter 6, you learned how to use commas with compound and complex sentences. Now you will learn more punctuation rules.

End Punctuation

End punctuation is exactly what it sounds like. It is the punctuation that goes at the end of a sentence.

There are three common punctuation marks that can end a sentence.

A **period** comes after a complete statement.

I am going swimming today**.**

My favorite food is pizza**.**

A **period** also follows a command.

Please take out the trash**.**

Come to the table and eat**.**

A **question mark** comes after any question.

Will you take me with you**?**

How much does the new Jonas Brothers CD cost**?**

An **exclamation point** follows an emotional or forceful statement.

Hey**!** That's a great idea**!**

Ouch**!** You stepped on my toe**!**

Commas in Addresses

Commas are used in many ways. In chapter 6, you saw some ways to use them in sentences. Another place where they are needed is in addresses.

Commas are used to **separate parts of an address**. A comma goes between the city and the state. If the sentence goes on after the state, put another comma after it.

Example: Mrs. Corrigan is from Tulsa**,** Oklahoma**,** and moved to Louisiana last year.

In a full address, there are more commas. One goes after the street name. Another goes after the town or city name.

Example: 2913 Pickle Lane, Sawyer, OH 42301

Commas and Quotation Marks

You read about direct quotation earlier in this chapter. Writers use **commas and quotation marks** to show when people are speaking. Quotation marks show where the quote begins and ends. Use them in pairs. One quotation mark goes before the quote. The other goes after it. Periods and commas go *inside* the second quotation mark.

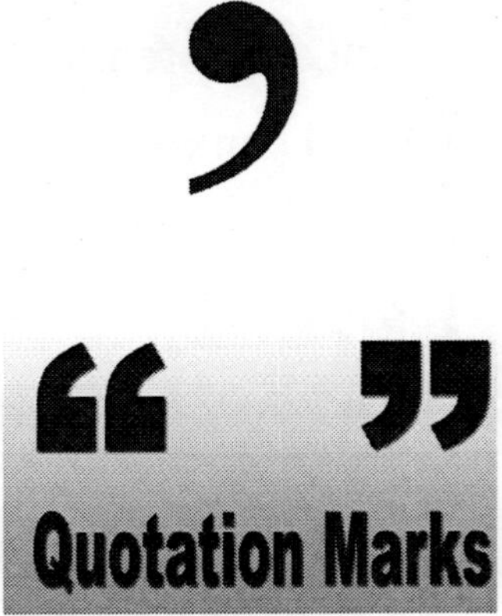

Examples: Austin says, "I like the way she sings."

"It's time to play outside," said Grandpa.

Chapter 9

Apostrophes

An **apostrophe** is needed to show possession.

That is Mary's sweater.

This is my parents' car.

Using an **apostrophe** shows who owns the object in the sentence. The sweater belongs to Mary, so it is Mary's sweater. The car belongs to my parents, so it is my parents' car. In the second sentence, the apostrophe is put after the *s*. This is because it refers to more than one parent, and *parents* is plural. In this case, the apostrophe goes after the *s*.

Practice 2: Punctuation

L 2.b–d (DOK 1–2)

Read the passage. It contains mistakes. Then answer the questions about it.

Kids' World Magazine

1187 Beecher Road Miami FL 33134

To the editor:

You should have more photo's in your magazine. The articles' are fun.

But you need to show what they talk about. I read one article about ants. It told me about anthills, which are the ants' homes. It said "Anthills are where the ants live and store their food". But there was no picture of an anthill. It would be great to see how big anthill's are. Pictures would be very helpful. Could you please include more illustrations.

Thank you for listening.

Yours truly,

Torean James

1 How should the address be correctly punctuated?

A 1187 Beecher Road, Miami, FL 33134

B 1187 Beecher Road Miami FL 33134

C 1187, Beecher Road, Miami, FL 33134

D 1187 Beecher Road, Miami FL 33134

2 Which is the only sentence that uses an apostrophe correctly?

A You should have more photo's in your magazine.

B The articles' are fun.

C It told me about anthills, which are the ants' homes.

D It would be great to see how big anthill's are.

3 Which sentence needs to end with a question mark?

A I read one article about ants.

B But there was no picture of an anthill.

C Pictures would be very helpful.

D Could you please include more illustrations.

4 What is the correct way to write this sentence?

A It said "Anthills, are where the ants live, and store their food".

B It said, "Anthills are where the ants live and store their food."

C It said "Anthills are where the ants live and store their food,".

D It said, "Anthills are where the ants live and store their food"!

Chapter 9

USAGE

Usage means how you use the English language. There is a proper way to speak and write. It is called Standard English. To speak and write correctly, you need to pay attention to the rules you have learned.

CHOOSING WORDS AND PHRASES

Writers and speakers **choose words and phrases for effect**. You can do the same. You read in chapter 5 about shades of meaning. There are words and phrases that are just right to explain what you want people to know. You need to pick the right ones. Look at these examples.

Example 1: The comet zooms across the sky at night. It is bright, so you can see it from earth. It can help you tell direction. Watch it travel across the sky.

Example 2: The comet walks a path through the sky at night. It shines as bright as a spotlight. It is a guide through the dark. Follow the comet with me.

Both examples give the same facts. But Example 2 uses words and phrases for effect. For example, the author makes the comet seem to come alive by saying it "walks a path." Comparing it to a spotlight puts a picture in your mind of how bright it is. Finally, the author invites you to follow the comet. This pulls you right into the text.

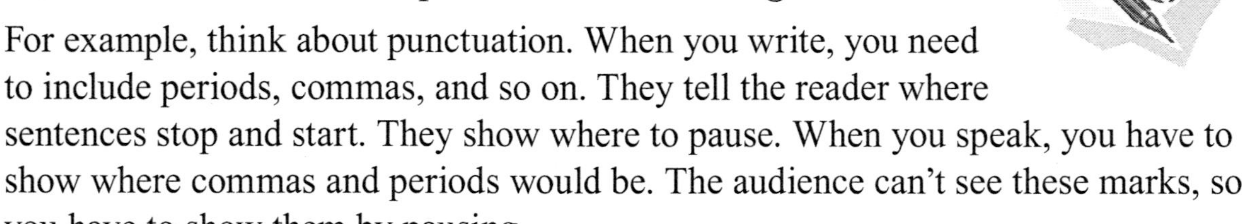

Here is another idea to keep in mind. Think about how you talk. Then think about how you write. Your language may be a bit different for the two tasks. You read about some rules at the start of this chapter. They are called conventions. Well, there are some **different conventions for spoken and written English**.

For example, think about punctuation. When you write, you need to include periods, commas, and so on. They tell the reader where sentences stop and start. They show where to pause. When you speak, you have to show where commas and periods would be. The audience can't see these marks, so you have to show them by pausing.

In writing, when you talk about a new topic, you can start a new paragraph. In speaking, the audience can't see that. So, you need to tell them. You need to include more transitions. You might say, "Now I will tell you about…" This helps introduce the new topic.

When you speak, you might include some extra words. You might also go on and on in what seems like one long sentence. Look at this example from a speech that Rodney made.

> So, once I got the game console, I had to go home and hook it all up. And, um, I had to add an extra cord so it could get plugged in, you know, into the wall, because it was too far from the plug. So then I read the instructions and booted it up and got it registered and everything and then I could finally start playing.

Do you see the extra words like *so* and *um*? There are also extra phrases like *you know* and *and everything*? People often add these when they speak. When you hear a speech like this, it sounds fine. You get the facts that Rodney is telling you. But in writing, the ideas would look a bit different. Rodney would need to use conventions of written English. The same example might look like thi

> When I got the game console, I had to go home and hook it all up. I had to add an extra cord so it could get plugged into the wall because the console was too far from the electric socket. Then I read the instructions and booted it up. I got it registered, and then I could finally start playing.

Did you notice what else changed? In writing, Rodney made separate sentences out of the long ramble in his speech. Now, he has complete and correct sentences. He also replaced the word *plug*. He found a more precise phrase—*electric socket.*

Practice 3: Usage

W 2.a–d, **L** 3.a, b (DOK 3)

What do you want to do when you grow up? Write a letter to ask about the job you want to have in the future. It could be to a person who has that job. It could be to the kind of company that offers the job you want.

Write your letter on your own paper. Be sure to do the following:

- Find the address for the person or company you want to write (or make one up). Include it at the top of the letter.
- Use correct capitalization.
- Use correct punctuation.
- Choose the best words and phrases for effect.

Activity

SL 4, 5, **L** 3

After writing your letter for Practice 3, make it into a speech. Start with an introduction like, "If I could talk to this person, here is what I would ask." Be sure to use the conventions for spoken English. This means including pauses to show where sentences begin and end. It also means using transitions to tell your audience when you start a new topic. Make your speech interesting and lively.

You could also make an audio recording of your speech. Then, listen to how different the speech sounds from the written letter.

Chapter 9 Summary

Capitalize these words:

- the **word *I***
- names of **days** and **months**
- **proper names**, like *Macy*, *Keith*, and *Aunt Linda*
- **proper places**, like *Cambodia*, *Louisiana*, and *Breckinridge Elementary School*
- **titles** of books, songs, magazines, poems, and so on
- the first word in **direct quotations**

Punctuation organizes the ideas in a passage.

End punctuation helps show how to read a sentence.

Commas have many rules. They are used to **separate parts of an address** and with **quotation marks** to show when people are speaking. Quotation marks show where a person's spoken words begin and end.

An **apostrophe** is used to show possession.

Usage means how you use the English language.

- Writers and speakers **choose words and phrases for effect**.
- There are some **different conventions for spoken and written English**.

Chapter 9 Review

L 2.a–d, 3.a, b (DOK 1–2)

DIRECTIONS **Read the passage. It contains mistakes. Then answer the questions.**

1 A fire engine roared down Elm street. It rounded the corner and came to a stop. It was right in front of 229 Beech Street Howellville Kentucky. That is Amandas' house! Amanda is my friend and a really nice girl.

2 The firefighters rushed in. Smoke came out the back of the house. Was it going to burn down completely. More firemen attached the hose to the hydrant on the corner. They started spraying the house with water. They all looked like real pros. None of the firefighters even looked scared.

3 My mom and I were standing in front of our house down the street. I saw Amanda and her family standing a few houses away. We went over to talk to them. They were scared and sad. I hugged Amanda. "Don't worry" I told her. "The firefighters will save your house. And the best thing is that no one was hurt." Amanda smiled a little and nodded.

4 Soon the fire was out. There was really not much damage. Just one room was really smoky—and now wet, thanks to the fire hoses. To be safe, Amanda and her mom, brothers, and sisters stayed at her aunts house for a couple of nights. Over the next few days, we all helped clean up. Now the family is back in the house, and the sirens seem like a bad dream!

1 What is the correct way to write the first sentence?

A A fire engine roared down elm street.

B A Fire engine roared down Elm street.

C A fire engine roared down Elm Street.

D A Fire Engine roared down Elm Street.

2 What is the correct way to write the third sentence?

A It was right in front of, 229 Beech Street, Howellville Kentucky.

B It was right in front of 229, Beech Street, Howellville Kentucky.

C It was, right in front of 229 Beech Street, Howellville Kentucky.

D It was right in front of 229 Beech Street, Howellville, Kentucky.

Read the fourth sentence.

That is Amandas' house!

3 What is the correct way to write the underlined word?

A Amanda

B Amanda's

C Amandas's

D Correct as is

4 Which sentence from paragraph 2 needs to end with a question mark?

A The firefighters rushed in.

B Smoke came out the back of the house.

C Was it going to burn down completely.

D They started spraying the house with water.

Read this sentence from paragraph 3.

"Don't worry" I told her.

5 What is the correct way to write this sentence?

A "Don't worry," I told her.

B "Don't, worry," I told her.

C "Don't worry". I told her.

D "Don't worry." I told her.

Chapter 9

Read this sentence from the last paragraph.

To be safe, Amanda and her mom, brothers, and sisters stayed at her aunts house for a couple of nights.

6 Which word in the sentence needs an apostrophe?

A brothers

B sisters

C aunts

D nights

Chapter 10
Speaking and Listening

This chapter covers DOK levels 1–3 and the following third grade strands and standards (for full standards, please see Appendix A):

Speaking and Listening: 1–6

Classroom Discussion

In your class, you may be asked to read stories or other texts that you will later discuss. You may be asked to talk about them with your teacher, classmates, or a group. **Discussion** helps you to understand what you read. You can hear views and opinions of others. They might be different from your own views. You can ask questions and answer questions as you discuss. This also gives you a chance to express your ideas clearly.

Preparation

It is important to know how to **prepare for discussions**. Here are a few things that you can do to prepare.

Read the Required Text

Read the required text that your teacher assigned. You need to read it carefully and slowly. This will help you to make sure you understand what you read. Taking notes, asking questions, and rereading are all strategies that can help you comprehend what you are reading.

Research the Topic

You can find out more about a topic by doing some **research**. (You will read more about research in chapter 11.) For example, say you are reading a book about whales. You can look up whales in an encyclopedia to learn even more about them. You can even do research when reading a story. You could find out more about the author or the setting. This will help you add more facts in your class discussion.

Make Notes about What You Learn

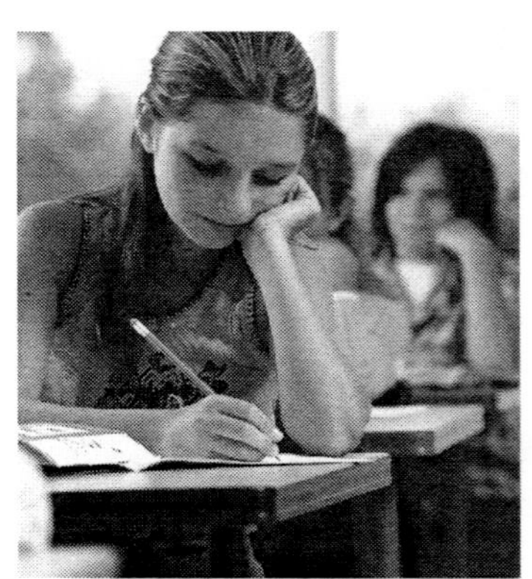

As you read and research, you can **take notes**. Make some notes about these items:

- Main idea of the text
- Details that support the main idea
- Answers to questions you ask yourself
- Ideas you have about the meaning of the text
- Questions you still have after reading

Follow Rules of Discussion

There are some **rules of discussion** that everyone should follow. These rules may be set by your teacher or by the class. They allow a group to work well together. They help the discussion to go smoothly, so no one hurts classmates' feelings or is rude.

Rules for discussion might look like this:

Rule 1. **Talk to others in a respectful way. Raise your hand, and wait for your turn.**

Rule 2. **Listen to others with care. Make eye contact and pay attention to what each speaker is saying.**

Rule 3. **Speak one at a time. Do not talk while others are talking.**

Rule 4. **Stay on the topic. Only speak about the text you are discussing. If someone asks a question, try to answer it before asking another question.**

Rule 5. **Explain your ideas in a way others will understand.**

Practice 1: Classroom Discussion

SL 1 (DOK 1)

DIRECTIONS **Read and then answer the questions.**

1 Which of the following is appropriate preparation for class discussion?

A Ask your classmates their opinions of the text.

B Read the text carefully, and do some research.

C Write an essay on the topic to give your teacher.

D Skim the text quickly, and write some questions.

2 What should you do when your classmate or the teacher is speaking?

A Read your book.

B Have a conversation with your partner.

C Make eye contact and listen quietly.

D Argue with his or her idea.

3 When listening to a report or speech, what are the most important parts to remember?

A The facts you did not know

B The title of the speech

C The main idea and details

D The concluding sentence

Listening

When a person talks in class, be sure to look at the speaker. You should pay close attention so you can understand the topic.

Listening Comprehension

In school, you will spend time listening to others speak or read. When you listen, think about what you hear. Determine the **main idea and supporting details** of what the speaker says or reads. You need to listen carefully to do that. You might need to take notes too.

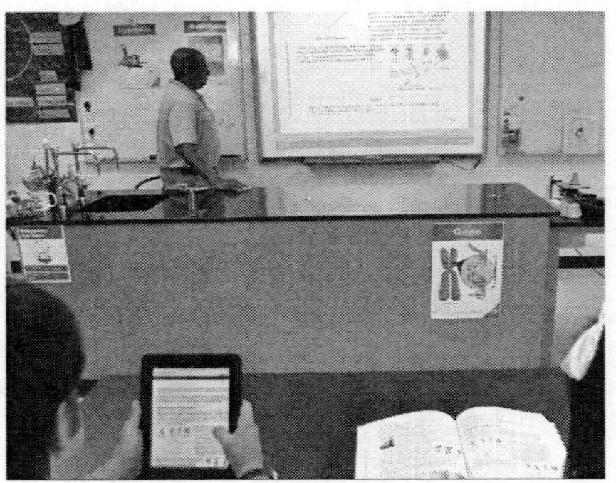

If there are parts you do not understand, make a note. You can make a note on paper or in your head. You will usually have a chance to ask your questions at the end of the speech.

Asking Questions

Asking questions about a speech can help you understand it better. You can ask the speaker a question about the topic. But be sure it is really about the topic! Also, it might turn out that another student in class has an answer. And you might be able to answer questions that others ask.

In class discussion, you can add what you know. When all students share, each one gets to know the topic better. Talking about a speech or report is like any other class discussion. Remember to wait until it is your turn to talk.

Practice 2: Listening

SL 2, 3 (DOK 1, 3)

DIRECTIONS **Please ask your teacher or another adult to read the next passage aloud. Then answer the questions that follow.**

Hat History

Do you wear a hat or cap when you go out? If so, you are following in the footsteps of your ancestors. Many historians believe head coverings can be traced back as far as the cave dwellers. These early hats were not just fashion. They were a way to protect heads from bad weather. However, by ancient times, hats came to symbolize a person's rank in life. Ancient Greeks and Romans made felt from sheep's wool. They used the wool to make a simple skull cap. The cap could only be worn by free men. When a Greek or Roman slave was given his freedom, he was presented with one of these "liberty caps."

By the 1600s, hats also showed the man's sense of style. In addition to felt, hats were made of fur or straw. The closely fitting caps were replaced by hats with crowns as high as seven inches. Over time, the height of the crown changed. So did the width of the brim. Men were always looking for new head coverings that were practical but stylish.

From early times, women kept their heads covered in public. Veils, scarves, hoods, and simple caps served that purpose. When they did begin wearing hats, the hat designs were based on men's hats. In the late 1600s, this changed. Hat makers began making styles just for women. This was a great time for women. Women's hats became an important part of fashion.

Many kinds of caps and hats are popular today. People still wear hats to protect against the weather. They also wear them to make a fashion statement.

1 Who wore a "liberty cap"?

A A Greek or Roman freed slave

B A woman who was very independent

C A Greek or Roman who owned slaves

D A person who liked getting items for free

2 Which types of hats appeared first?

A Hats made of straw or animal fur

B Veils that covered the head and face

C Large hats with feathers and ribbons

D Closely fitting caps with small brims

3 What is the best summary of this selection?

____

____

____

____

SPEAKING

You might need to give a report in class. It could be a **report on a topic** you researched. Or you might **tell a story** about something that happened to you.

If you need to give a report, be sure to do research. You should know as much as possible about your topic. You might not include it all in your speech. But if others ask questions, you will know how to answer them.

In giving a report or telling a story, give the ideas in order. Tell them in a way that those listening can follow easily. Be sure to give enough details. Describe the people, places, and events carefully.

Whatever you need to speak about, here are some things you will want to do:

- Stay on the topic.
- Include facts and details.
- Speak clearly and at a good pace—not too slow, and not too fast.
- Use complete sentences.
- Make eye contact with your audience.
- After the speech, answer questions from the audience.

Chapter 10

Sound Recording

In school, you might make a **sound recording** as you read a text. The teacher may ask you to read a story or a poem. A recording can help you hear how well you read aloud. When you read aloud, think about doing these things:

- Read smoothly, the way you would talk.
- Pause at the end of each sentence, rather than running right into the next sentence.
- Speak at a speed that listeners can follow.
- Don't mumble. Speak clearly so that people can understand what you say.
- Pay attention to what you are reading. Let your voice reflect the text. For example, if you read a scary part of a story, let your voice show it is scary.

Visual Displays

When you present, you can use **visuals** too. They can help you clearly express your topic and ideas. Graphs, posters, charts, and pictures can be used along with your speech. Graphs and charts are useful to present data and facts. Pictures and posters can help illustrate a story. You can use printed graphics or show graphics on a computer.

For example, if you were telling your classmates how to check out a book from the library, you could include a flow chart like this.

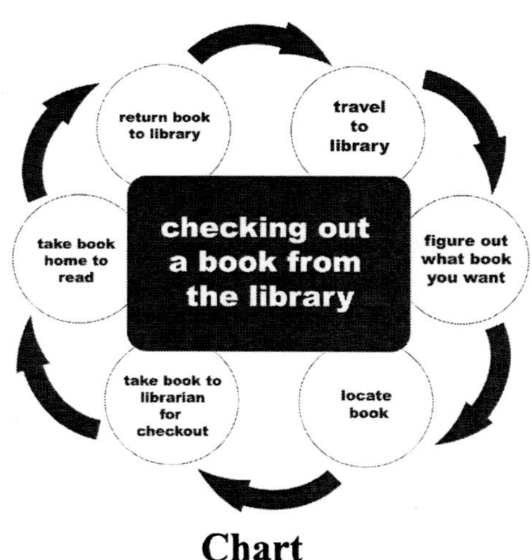

Chart

Practice 3: Speaking

SL 4–6 (DOK 1–3)

DIRECTIONS **Read and then answer the questions.**

1 When presenting a report, what should you do?

A Stay on the topic of the report.

B Talk about anything that comes to mind.

C Ask your classmates as many questions as you can.

D Have a study partner come up with you and speak too.

2 Why is it helpful to record yourself speaking, and then listen to how you sound? How can this help you in making speeches in class?

____

____

____

____

3 Kayla will present a report about how animals spend the winter. She will include how some hibernate (sleep through the cold months) and how others adapt or migrate (move to warmer areas). She wants to use a visual to support her speech. Which of the following is the best visual for Kayla to use?

A A table that shows which animals live in cold climates

B A photograph of bears hibernating in their den

C A chart of year-round migration patterns of geese

D A map showing the places where winter gets coldest

4 Kayla wants to add facts about how squirrels store food for winter. She wants to show how this is one way to adapt. Which of the following is the best way for her to say this?

A Squirrels like nuts. They put them in holes in trees. I wonder how many nuts they can keep in there.

B Some animals don't hibernate. Squirrels, they stay active. They eat food they saved.

C Have you ever watched a squirrel? It runs around looking for food all the time. It always seems hungry.

D Some animals, like squirrels, adapt by storing food in fall. In winter, they eat the stored nuts and seeds.

Activity

W 1.a–d, 2.a–d, 7, **SL** 4

Prepare a short report (3 to 5 minutes). Present it in class or to a group. Be sure to do the following:

1 Make sure all of your facts are clear and relevant.

2 Give details and describe things well.

3 Speak clearly.

4 Use complete sentences.

5 Include appropriate visuals.

Choose a topic to talk about, or you can pick one of these:

- How a rainbow appears
- My favorite painting or sculpture
- The job of an elected official (president, governor, and so on)
- Why people first came to America
- My favorite book or story
- The roots of modern music (pick one type of music)
- How a character changes in a book or movie
- The best place in the world to live
- Which animal has the best eyesight
- The most interesting sport
- Ways to study space
- Who is the best superhero, and why

Chapter 10 Summary

Classroom discussion helps you to understand what you read.

Read the required text. Come to class **prepared** to discuss what you read.

Research the topic. **Take notes** about what you learn.

Ask and try to answer relevant **questions**.

Follow the **rules of discussion**, such as waiting for your turn to speak.

Determine the **main idea** and **supporting details** of a text read aloud.

Create interesting **recordings of texts** that show your reading skills.

When you report on a topic, use appropriate **visuals**.

Chapter 10 Review

SL 1–6 (DOK 1–3)

DIRECTIONS **Read and then answer the questions.**

1 Which of these is the best way to show you are listening to a speaker?

A Nodding to show you understand

B Eating snacks while you listen

C Tapping your foot to a beat in your head

D Patting the speaker on the shoulder

2 Why is it important to make eye contact with a speaker?

A It makes you remember the color of the speaker's eyes.

B It shows the speaker that you are not falling asleep.

C It helps you to focus on what the speaker is saying.

D It means you can see the speaker, so he or she can see you.

3 A person is telling you something important. What is the best way to ask questions?

A Interrupt the speaker when you have a question.

B Wait for a pause, and then ask your questions.

C Look around to show you are ready to talk.

D Write down questions, and e-mail them later.

4 Laila is giving a speech about her vacation to Hawaii. While she was there with her family, she visited the Dole pineapple plantation, saw the Pearl Harbor Memorial, and even went surfing! She wants to include a visual aid to help tell about her trip. Choose which of the following visuals would be the best for her to include, and explain your answer on the lines below.

A

C

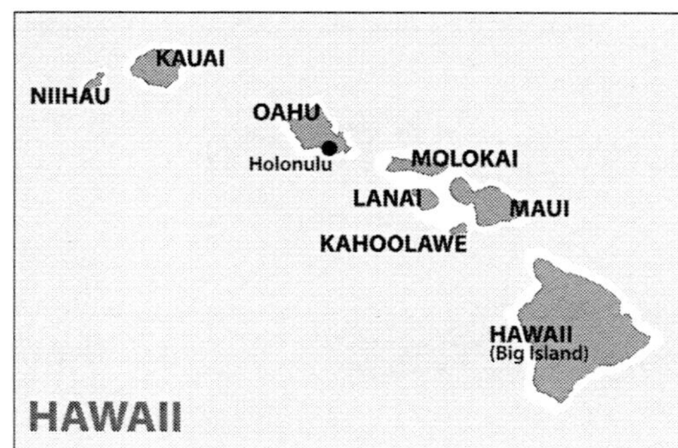

B

D

____

____

____

Chapter 11
Research

This chapter covers DOK levels 1–3 and the following third grade strands and standards (for full standards, please see Appendix A):

Writing: 7, 8
Speaking and Listening: 1.a

Looking for facts is called **research**. In chapter 10, you read about doing research to find out more about a topic. Doing research builds on what you know about a topic. When you research a topic, you can read about it in a book. You can use a computer. You can ask an expert. These are all ways to research a topic.

Information Sources

An **information source** is something you use to find facts. Sources are what you use to do research. Say you have to do a report about bugs. You have to choose the bug to write about. Then you have to find out facts that you can report. You need sources!

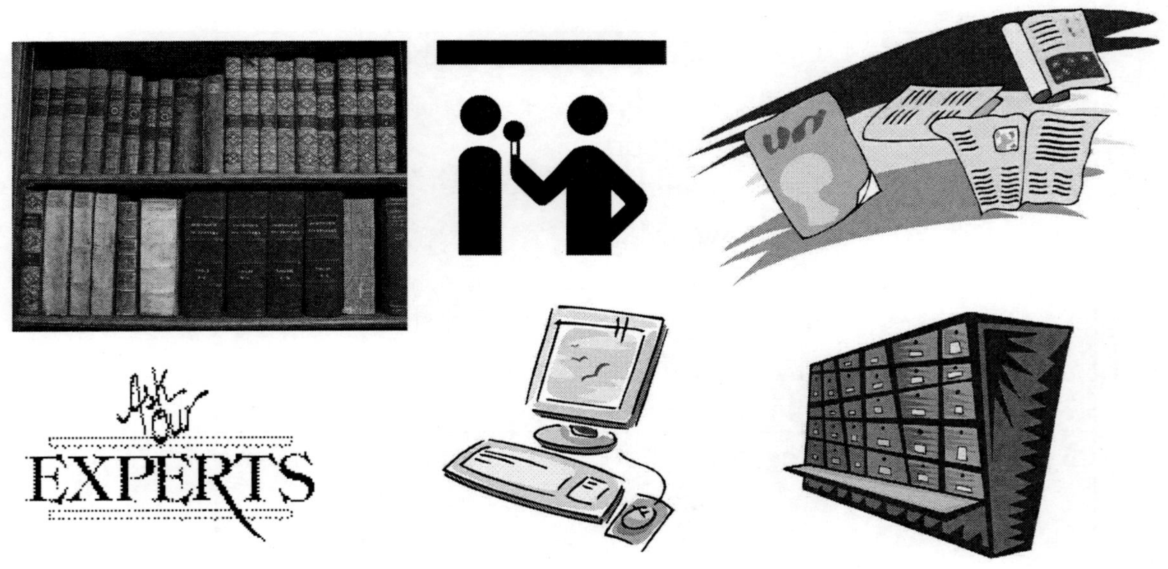

Chapter 11

Print Sources

Print sources include books, magazines, and so on. You can use the library catalog to find books.

Print Information Sources		
Source	**What's in It**	**Example**
Atlas	An **atlas** is a book of maps. It also has facts about countries. It might have charts, tables, and text about people, climate, resources, and history. Atlases are usually bigger than other books. This is because they contain detailed maps that don't fit well on small pages.	*Hammond Atlas of the World*
Encyclopedia	**Encyclopedias** have facts about many topics. You can find them in the library or on the Internet. They have articles on many subjects. This includes people, places, historical events, science, and technology. The articles are in ABC order by topic.	*Children's Encyclopedia of American History*
Newspaper	**Newspapers** provide news about current events. They tell what's going on in the world and in your town. Many have sections on business, politics, the arts, crime, weather, ads, and editorials (articles that give opinions about issues).	*New York Times*
Magazine	**Magazines** have articles and ads. You can find magazines on many topics, including beauty, health, sports, fishing, cars, and so on.	*TIME for Kids*

Electronic Sources

Electronic sources are ones that you can find online. You can find facts about almost anything on the Internet (also called the World Wide Web). But you have to be careful. Anyone can put up a webpage. You need to check that the page has real facts. Some pages are written by experts. Those from a university or a government agency can be the best. These usually have facts. Chat pages or sites that sell things are not good sources to use.

Key Word Search

The best way to find a topic online is to use a **search engine**. Some popular search engines are Google, Yahoo!, and MSN. Each has a space where you can type in your topic. The engine does a **key word search** of what you typed. Key words should be specific.

Say that you decide your bug will be a beetle. If you use the key word *beetle*, you will get millions of pages! Some will be about the bugs, but others may be about pest control. Some may even be about the Volkswagen car! So be specific. Try *beetle insect*. Or pick one kind of beetle.

Other Sources

Besides print and online, there are **other sources** you can use. Audio and video also can be sources. For example, you might be writing about poetry. You could listen to a song on CD. Then you can write about how the song uses a literary device. Or you might look at a film about the Civil War. You could use facts from the film in a report for class.

Another source is a real live expert. Say that you want to make a speech about running as a sport. Your older brother is on the track team. You could interview him to get facts from a runner.

YOU are a source too! Everything you have read and done in your life gives you facts. Say you have to write a report about fish. You might think about pet fish you had. You can include what you know about how they eat and behave. This makes you a source.

Chapter 11

Which Is the Best Source?

Once you find sources, you have to **pick the best sources** to use. Some will be better for your topic than others. Ask yourself some questions:

- Who wrote this? Is the author an expert?
- Does it answer my questions?
- Does it give interesting facts I can use?
- Do I understand it all?

If you can answer yes to all of these, you likely have a good source!

Practice 1: Information Sources

W 7, 8, **SL** 1.a (DOK 1–2)

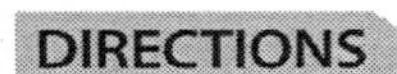

Look at the sources. Then answer the questions that follow.

1. From the Book, *Cartoon Characters Yesterday and Today*

Cartoon Characters
YESTERDAY and **Today**

vi

2. From the Book, *Cartoon Characters Yesterday and Today*

Bold entries include illustrations

3. Internet Website Information
cartoons-R-us.net

CARTOONS-R-US.NET

IT'S ALL ABOUT THE 'TOONS!

Find a 'toon! [ ] Search

old toons | new toons | comic strips | about | contact us

Speed Racer

One fun old cartoon is Speed Racer. It was adapted from a Japanese anime. It was on American TV in 1967 and '68. In 2008, a live-action movie was made about Speed Racer's adventures.

The characters are silly but fun to watch. Speed Racer is a young race car driver. He solves a lot of mysteries. Trixie is his girlfriend. He also has a pet monkey named Chim-Chim and a little brother named Spritle. Mom and Pops Racer are Speed's parents. They manage the racing team. Racer X is a mysterious rival who turns out to be Speed's brother!

To read more, click on the characters:

Speed Racer
Trixie
Spritle and Chim-Chim
Racer X

To visit the official Speed Racer Web site, click here.

1 In the book *Cartoon Characters Yesterday and Today*, where can you see a picture of the Road Runner?

A Page 27 **B** Page 28 **C** Page 29 **D** Page 30

2 In which chapter would you look for information about Daffy Duck, a character who was in some cartoons with Bugs Bunny?

A Chapter 1 **B** Chapter 2 **C** Chapter 3 **D** Chapter 4

3 What would be the best page to start reading to find out about Snoopy?

A Page 18 **B** Page 26 **C** Page 36 **D** Page 38

4 What would you most likely do to learn more about Speed Racer?

A Read the book *Cartoon Characters Yesterday and Today.*

B Search the TV listings for reruns of the old cartoons.

C Go to the bookstore to see if they have Speed Racer comics.

D Click on the link to the official Speed Racer website.

5 Which of these websites would you click on to read more about Mickey Mouse's pet dog, Pluto?

A Pluto - Wikipedia, the free encyclopedia
"Pluto is the second-largest known dwarf planet in the Solar System ..."
en.wikipedia.org/wiki/Pluto - Cached - Similar –

B Pluto
Oct 28, 2008 "... what we've learned about Pluto by Dr. Alan Stern of the New Horizons mission."
www.nineplanets.org.pluto.html - Cached - Similar –

C Disney Archives | Pluto Character History
"Relive Disney's remarkable and memorable past with Pluto in the Disney Archives."
disney.go.com/vault/archives/.../pluto/pluto.html - Cached - Similar –

D Pluto's Restaurant, Fresh Food for a Hungry Universe
"Welcome to Pluto's Restaurant, serving fresh wholesome salads, sandwiches …" www.plutosfreshfood.com - Cached - Similar –

6 What key word search would most likely help you learn about which cartoon characters people like today?

A Famous cartoons

B Popular cartoons today

C TV cartoons

D What are the best cartoons?

Chapter 11

Using Sources

So, what do you do with a source once you find it? You use it! What you learn from sources helps you know your topic. Your papers and reports can mention what you found out. In this section, we'll talk about **using sources**. This includes how to take notes and organize your facts.

You use sources to find facts for reports and essays. You can also use sources to make sure you are ready for class discussions.

Take Notes

When you read sources, you can't remember all the facts they give you. A good way to hang on to the facts you need is to **take notes**. Use a journal or note cards to jot down any information you might want to use. Here is an example.

Jordan is writing his report on bugs. (Remember the topic from earlier?) The bug he picked is the soldier beetle. Here is an article he found about it.

Soldier Beetle, Family Cantharidae

Counteracts these pest(s):

Aphid

How to recognize

Approximately 1/2 inch in length, the adult soldier beetle has a narrow, black abdomen and bright red head or thorax. The soldier beetle larva is various shades of orange with black markings.

Benefits

Soldier beetles prey upon aphids, caterpillars, grasshopper eggs and beetle larvae, among other insects around the garden.

How to attract

Since some soldier beetles feed on nectar, you may be able to attract them with flowering plants.

Fun fact

Soldier beetles are nicknamed leatherwings because of their soft, cloth-like wing covers.

Source: http://www.govlink.org/hazwaste/house/yard/problems/goodbugs

Jordan was at school when he found this on the Internet. He could not print the page. So he took some notes. Look at the facts he wrote down.

Soldier beetle
Cantharidae
1/2 inch long, black and red
eats aphids, caterpillars, other garden pests
plant flowers to attract them
soft wings - nickname leatherwings

See how easy that was? Jordan wrote just a few important words and phrases. These will help him when he writes his report.

When you take notes, also write down where the facts came from. You will need this later. If you write a composition, you need to give credit to your sources. Later in this chapter, you will see how to do that.

Organize Your Facts

A good way to organize is to **make an outline**. It helps you put the facts in order. In an outline, you put your main ideas as the headings. The supporting details go underneath. They are called subheadings. Here is an example of an outline format.

Topic

I. Point 1 (Heading)

- A. First subpoint for Point 1 (Subheading)
- B. Second subpoint for Point 1 (Subheading)

II. Point 2 (Heading)

- A. First subpoint for Point 2 (Subheading)
- B. Second subpoint for Point 2 (Subheading)

When you read a text, making an outline will also help you understand the topics. Each chapter title would be the main heading. The important ideas in that chapter would be the subheadings.

Here is Jordan's outline for his report on the soldier beetle. He used the notes he made about the article he found. He also used facts from other sources.

Jordan's Outline

I. Soldier beetle
   A. One kind of beetle (there are millions)
   B. Black with red markings (like a uniform)
   C. Called leatherwing because of soft wings

II. Where it lives
   A. North America
   B. Europe
   C. Asia

III. What it eats
   A. Aphids
   B. Caterpillars
   C. Insect eggs and larvae

IV. Why it is good
   A. Eats garden pests
   B. Helps pollinate plants

See how the outline helps put each fact in the right place? Now Jordan has a logical way to give his report!

Practice 2: Using Sources

W 7, 8, **SL** 1.a (DOK 1–3)

DIRECTIONS **Suppose you want to find out more about animals that change from birth to adulthood. You want to write a report about this for science class. Here are three sources about this topic. Look at the sources. Then answer questions 1 through 4.**

1. Encyclopedia Article
"Life Cycle"

LIFE CYCLE

Life cycle is the term used to tell how a living thing is born, lives, and dies. Humans have two main stages of life. After growing in the mother for nine months, they are born as babies. Then, they slowly grow into adults.

Some mammals have life cycles like humans. They have babies, and those babies grow up into adults. One example is a blue whale. A blue whale has a baby whale (called a calf). Then, the calf grows up to be an adult blue whale.

Some animals are born as eggs, and then they hatch. For example, birds lay eggs. The eggs hatch, and the baby birds grow up into adult birds. Many reptiles, like snakes, begin as eggs too. Fish start out as eggs as well.

A mother swan and babies

Insects have a different kind of life cycle. They go through a process called metamorphosis. This means they change from one form into another. A butterfly is a good example of this. A butterfly begins as an egg. Then, it hatches into a larva. The larva grows into a caterpillar. The caterpillar makes a cocoon to stay in for a while. When it comes out, it is a beautiful butterfly.

141

2. Internet Website Information
http://www.frankiesmomblog.net.

"Finding a Tadpole"

frankiesmomblog.net

Archives

- December 2008
- January 2009
- February 2009
- March 2009
- April 2009
- May 2009
- June 2009
- July 2009
- August 2009

Finding a Tadpole (page 1)

I take Frankie to the pond every Saturday. He likes to throw rocks and look at all the pond creatures. It's so cute to watch him. Today, Frankie went to the edge of the pond. He saw a creature swimming around. Of course, he gets in the water to get a closer look. I see that it is a tadpole.

Frankie scoops up the baby frog. He wants it for his new pet. We take it home in a cup of lake water. We put the tadpole in an old fish-bowl. Then, I teach Frankie about the life of a frog. I draw him a picture to explain. It didn't look very nice. (I'm no artist!) I tell him that soon the tadpole will grow into a frog, and Frankie will have a pet frog. After we talk about that, I boil some lettuce so Frankie can feed his tadpole.

Frankie asks me how long it will take for his tadpole to become a frog. I tell him it could take a few months. He makes me laugh because he decides he does not want to wait so long for the tadpole to be a frog. I tell him to be patient because pretty soon, the tadpole will sprout legs. Then, it will lose its tail. Finally, it will be a frog!

Here is a prettier version of the frog life cycle I drew for Frankie!

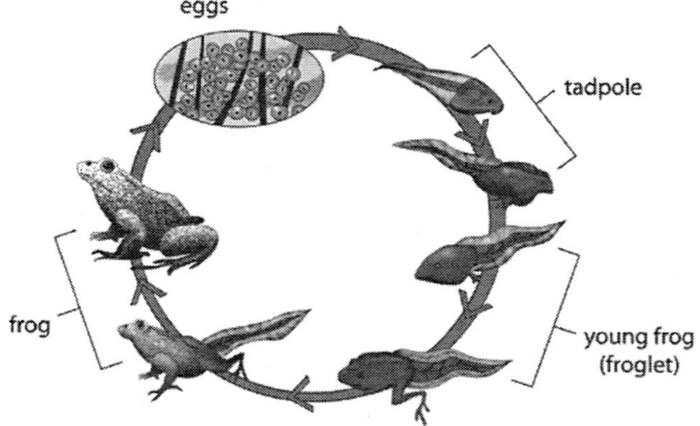

3. Excerpts from the Book, *Learning about Insect Life Cycles*

a. Copyright Page

Learning about Insect Life Cycles

Artwork by Poplar Design Studio

Cover Photo: Leon James

Published by:
Imperial Press
401 Grant St.
New York, NY
United States of America

Copyright © 2008 by Alyssa Holder
All rights reserved. Printed in the United States of America. Except as permitted under the United States Copyright Act, no part of this publication may be reproduced, stored, or retransmitted in any form without prior written permission of the publisher.

iii

Copyright © American Book Company

Chapter 11

1 According to the blog entry "Finding a Tadpole," what must happen before the tadpole becomes a froglet?

A It has to lose its tail.

B It has to hatch its egg.

C It has to sprout legs.

D It has to breathe under water.

2 In the butterfly life cycle, what must happen before a larva can be born?

A A caterpillar must come out of a cocoon.

B A caterpillar needs to eat a lot of food.

C A butterfly has to build a cocoon.

D A butterfly has to lay some eggs.

3 Frankie wants to make an outline from the frog life cycle his mom made for him. Which stage of life would go in the blank for the outline below?

I. Egg

II. ________

III. Froglet

IV. Frog

4 According to the article "Life Cycles," which of the following animals would not begin as an egg?

A Penguin

B Lizard

C Tuna

D Dog

Your next assignment might be a report about space. For question 5, read this source about the Milky Way. Then make notes about what you read.

The Milky Way Galaxy

The Milky Way is not just the name of a candy bar. It is our galaxy. The Milky Way is a huge spiral galaxy. This means it looks like a large pinwheel. It includes the sun and the earth and other planets.

The galaxy includes 200 billion stars. Some stars are too far away to be seen with the eye. People must use powerful telescopes. The stars that can be seen in the sky are ones that lie close to the solar system. They can be seen without a telescope, like the North Star and the Big Dipper.

Scientists believe that the Milky Way is 14 billion years old. It contains young, blue, so-called type I stars. It also contains the older, red, type II stars. Some scientists who study stars think that in the center of the Milky Way is a really big black hole. The Milky Way is a source of endless study.

5 Make some notes about the facts in this source. Look back at the note card example in this chapter. Remember to include the main idea and important details.

Chapter 11 Summary

An **information source** is something you use to do research and find answers.

Printed sources include books, magazines, brochures, and so on. You can use the library catalog to find books.

Electronic sources are ones that you can find online. To find webpages, use a **search engine** and enter a **keyword search**.

Other sources include audio and video.

You need to be able to **pick the best sources** to use for your topic.

When you find sources, a good way to keep the facts you need is to **take notes**.

A **summary** is a short way to tell what you read or heard.

A good way to organize facts about your topic is to **make an outline**.

Chapter 11 Review

W 7, 8, **SL** 1.a (DOK 1–3)

DIRECTIONS **A. Read and then answer the questions.**

1 Wesley wants to write about volcanoes in the United States. Which article would be best to use for research?

A "Kinds of Volcanoes"

B "Volcanoes in America"

C "Volcano Diagrams"

D "Why Volcanoes Erupt"

2 Kayla is writing a report about crops grown in Georgia. Which words would be best to type into a search engine?

A Georgia crops

B Georgia history

C crops in the South

D southern food

3 Kayla decides to narrow her topic to Georgia peaches. Which words would be best to type into a search engine?

A How to make peach jam

B How peaches taste

C Cotton, tobacco, and peaches

D Growing peaches in Georgia

DIRECTIONS **B. Look at this outline. Then, answer the questions about it.**

Reasons to Eat Fruit

I. Good for you

A. ____________________

B. Gives you energy

II. Satisfies Hunger

A. Has fiber

B. ____________________

1 Which best completes subheading I.A.?

A Is expensive

B Spoils fast

C Tastes bad

D Has vitamins

2 Which best completes subheading II.B.?

A More filling than junk food

B Oranges

C Has sugar

D Better than junk food

DIRECTIONS

C. Now choose one of the topics listed. Or think of your own topic. Then do some research in books and on the Internet. Ask your teacher, tutor, or librarian for help. Pick the best sources. Take notes about facts you find. You will use what you find in the next chapter. The chapter review at the end of chapter 12 will ask you to write about your topic.

Some Possible Research Topics

- The history of my favorite music
- An unusual fruit or vegetable
- How to take care of pet fish
- A place I would love to visit
- How a magic trick works
- Animals of the desert
- A fun outdoor activity
- A fun indoor activity
- Birds that can talk
- How to put on a play
- Hot air balloons
- Monorails

Chapter 12
Writing

This chapter covers DOK levels 1 and 3 and the following third grade strands and standards (for full standards, please see Appendix A):

Writing: 1–8, 10

You write almost every day. You might write notes or make lists of what you need to do. In school, you will need to write in different ways. This chapter has some ideas to help make your writing better.

Types of Writing

Before you start to write, ask yourself why you are writing. What is your purpose? All writing has a purpose, or reason. It might be to convince someone to do or think what you say. It could be to teach someone something new.

Tell Your Opinion

You might need to write what you think. For example, the teacher could ask you to pick the bravest character in a story. This means you have to **give your opinion**. You need to explain your point of view.

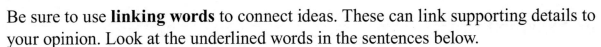

You can't just give an opinion. You want people to agree. So, you have to give reasons for your opinion. You must support what you think. This means including examples and details from the story. These details should show that you are right.

Be sure to use **linking words** to connect ideas. These can link supporting details to your opinion. Look at the underlined words in the sentences below.

Examples: Frodo was the bravest character <u>because</u> he went on even though he was scared.
<u>For example</u>, he said he would take care of the One Ring.

Give Information

You might also need to write **to inform or to explain**. The purpose is to teach your reader something. An example is a report you might write about volcanoes for the science fair.

This kind of writing needs to have many facts. You might also include definitions. Of course, you need good descriptions and details. Use linking words like "another," "both," and "but" so readers can see how facts relate to each other.

When you get ready to write, think about what you know. Focus on telling readers what they need to know. Use sources to learn more facts about your topic.

Create a Story

There are times when you will write to **tell a story**. When you write about a trip you went on, you are telling a story. This is also called **narrative writing**.

Narrative writing includes many details. It tells how things look, sound, smell, taste, and feel. A story should have good description. When you describe, you can use many adjectives and details. You want the reader to see, hear, smell, taste, and feel what is happening.

Be sure make your story interesting. Think about what details will make your story fun to read. To read more about parts of a story, review chapter 3.

Tell the events in an order that makes sense. Readers need to be able to follow along with what happens. Use linking words like "before," after," and "meanwhile" to tell when things happen.

How to Organize Your Writing

No matter what you will write about, you need to **organize your writing**. A written response has important parts. Here are the main parts that all your writing for school should have.

Introduction

In the **introduction**, you tell readers what your essay is about.

Example: Owls are fun to learn about. There are many kinds of owls all over the world.

Support

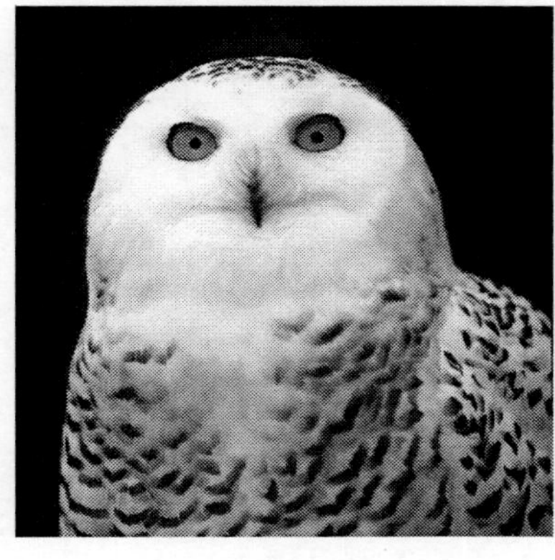

Now you need to **support** what you said in the introduction. You must **develop your topic**. This means adding details. These can be facts and examples.

Example: Owls are hunting birds. They are related to hawks. They hunt at night, so their big eyes can see well in the dark. Most birds have eyes on the sides of their head, but the owl's eyes are both in front. This gives them good depth perception (ability to judge distance). This is important for hunting small prey, like mice.

Conclusion

The **conclusion** is the last thing your reader sees. It is your last chance to make a point. Remind the reader of your main idea. Leave the reader with a final thought or question.

Example: Most people find owls interesting. In some cultures, they are symbols of wisdom. To me, they are just one of the coolest birds to study.

Steps of Writing

You know how to make a sandwich, right? First, you gather what you will use. You need bread and fillings. Then, you decide how you will put it together. Finally, you might add chips and a drink to make it complete.

Making a sandwich is a process. Writing is a process too. Here are the steps of the **writing process**. You should follow them when you write any composition.

The Writing Process	
Step	**What You Do**
Plan and Draft	Select a topic. Develop ideas. Write a draft.
Revise	Make sure ideas are clear. Add precise words and details.
Edit	Fix any errors.
Publish	Type your essay or report. Upload it for others to read.

Plan and Draft

The first step in writing an essay is **planning** what to write.

Select a Topic

Before you start to write, you have to **select a topic**. When you write for class, your teacher might tell you to pick any topic. Or, you may have a few subjects to choose from.

When you take a writing test, the writing prompt will give you a topic. But you still will need to decide exactly what you want to write. For example, look at this sample prompt.

> **A local radio show is having a writing contest. To enter, you need to write a story about having special powers, like a superhero, for one day. What kind of powers would you have? How would you use them?**
>
> **Before writing, think about superheroes and what they can do. How would your powers be special? What could you do in one day?**
>
> **Write a story about what you would do if you had superpowers for one day.**

The prompt gives you a topic. But you still need to decide a couple of things. What special powers will you have? What events will you tell about? In the next section, you will see ways to start thinking about what to write.

Do Some Prewriting

Prewriting means getting your ideas on paper. There are many ways to do this. Here are some easy ones. Ask your teacher about others.

Find the Facts

When you write for class, you may have time to look up some facts. Say that you want to have the powers that Spider-Man has. But you can't remember what they all are. You could **look it up** and see that Spider-Man is fast and strong. He also can climb walls and sense what is about to happen.

When you write for a test, you can't look up anything. But you can **use what you know**. What you already know can make great examples to support your ideas. For example, say you're writing about the superpowers you would have. You can explain them by telling which famous superheroes also have them. You could say, "I can fly like Superman and breathe under water like Aquaman. I also have a magic rope that makes people tell the truth, like Wonder Woman."

Use Brainstorming

Brainstorming is like thinking on paper. Think of a topic, and then list everything about it that pops into your head. After you do that for a few minutes, look over the list and pick the best ideas. Here is a sample based on the prompt about special powers.

Sample Brainstorming List

What powers would I have?
flying
invisible
walk through walls
hear or see really well
change into a creature
What would I do?
stop crime
show off to friends
help someone in need
have a superhero party

Chapter 12

Make a Graphic Organizer

A **graphic organizer** is a way to see how your ideas fit together. There are many kinds of graphic organizers. Some are better for narratives. Others will help you plan descriptive writing.

A **story map** is helpful for writing a narrative response. It can help you think about events. Here is a sample story map for a typical day.

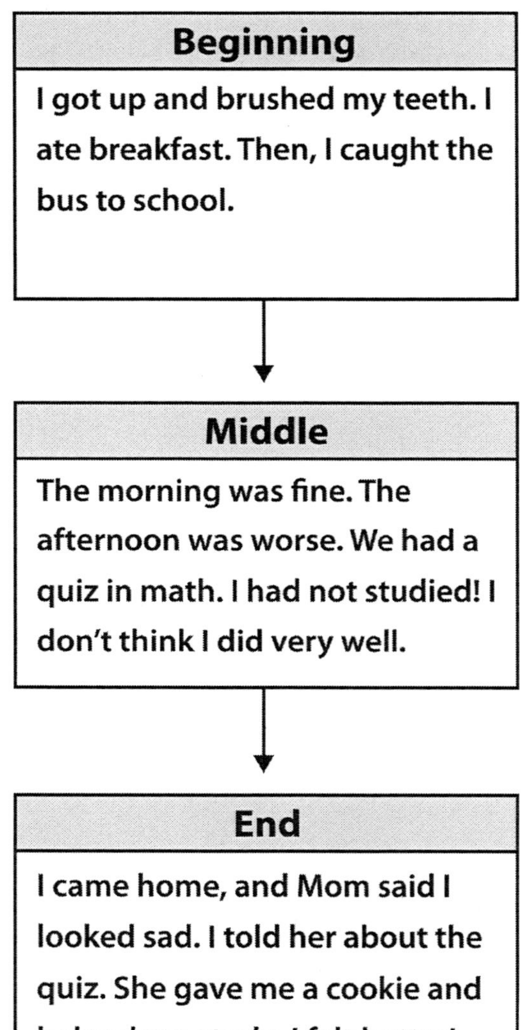

A **fishbone map** shows cause and effect. It has spaces for you to list what happens and why it happens. For example, if you are writing a story about falling off a bike, the fishbone map could look like this.

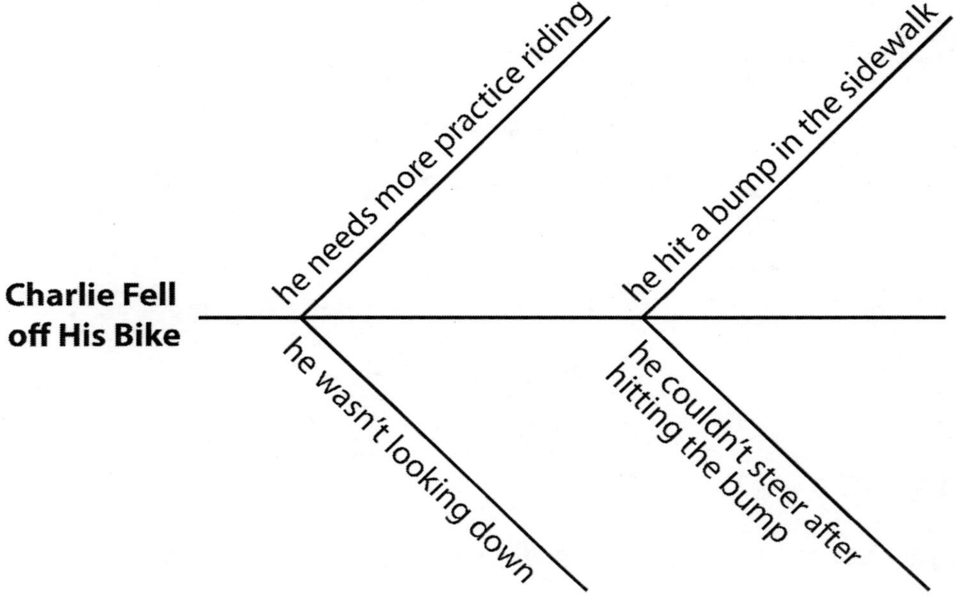

A **Venn diagram** is made up of two circles that overlap. It shows how two items are alike and different. The overlapping part of the circles has what is similar. Each separate circle has what goes with just that item. For example, say your topic is spiders and beetles. Your Venn diagram might look like this.

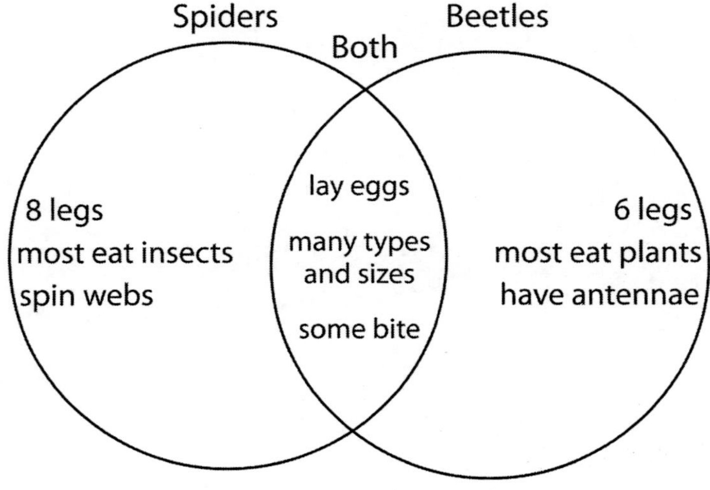

Webbing helps you develop a structure for your ideas. Your topic goes in the middle circle. Facts and examples go in other circles connected by lines to the middle circle.

What I Would Do with Superpowers

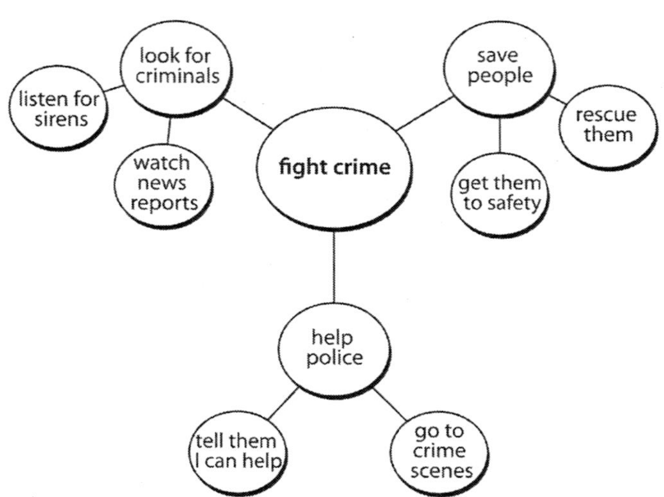

Write a Draft

It's time to get your ideas on paper. **Write a draft** using the ideas you came up with as you planned. When you draft, you should not worry about spelling or punctuation. But you should write in complete sentences. If some are not correct, that's all right. You will fix that later.

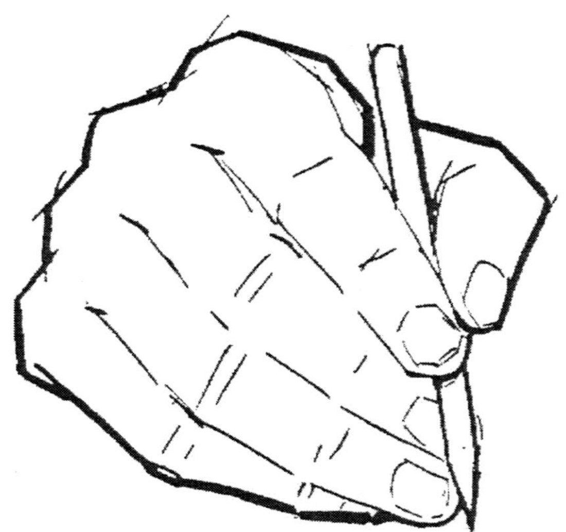

Practice 1: Planning and Drafting

W 1–5, 10 (DOK 1, 3)

DIRECTIONS **Read and then answer the following questions.**

Look at the graphic organizer Natalie made before writing her report.

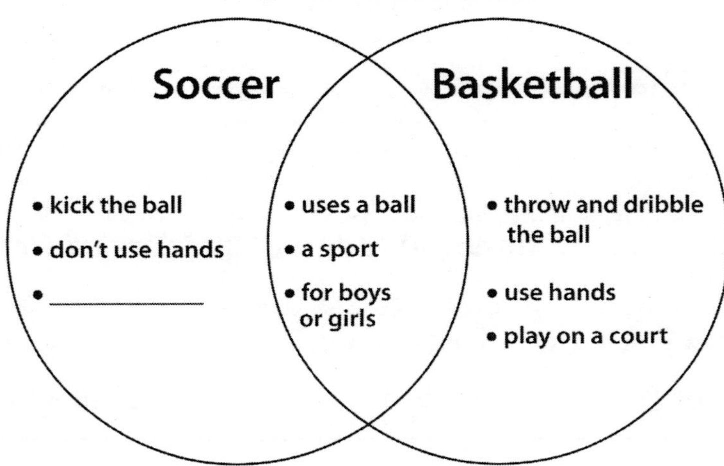

1 Which of these best fits in the empty space?

A two teams
B play on grass
C warm weather
D wear a uniform

Look at the graphic organizer John made before writing his report.

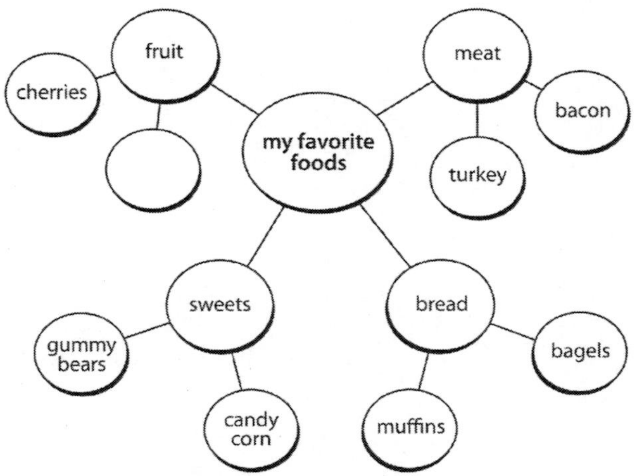

2 Which of these best fits in the empty space?

A chocolate **B** ham **C** bananas **D** rolls

3 Write about this prompt.

> **Write a story about something that happened that made you very happy.**
>
> **Use brainstorming or a graphic organizer to come up with ideas.**
>
> **Pick one idea that you want to write about.**
>
> **Use a graphic organizer or an outline to help put your ideas in order.**
>
> **Save your work. You will use it again for other practices in this chapter.**

4 Write about this prompt.

> **Describe the thing that you would most like to have if you could buy anything.**
>
> **Write some ideas. Use brainstorming or a graphic organizer to help you.**
>
> **Choose the idea you want to write about.**
>
> **Use a graphic organizer or an outline to help put your ideas in order.**

REVISE

You have a draft—good job! Now it's time improve your composition as much as you can. When you **revise**, you look for ways to improve what you wrote.

Revising for Clear Writing

Revising means improving your writing. In this step, you read your own work and look for ways to make it better. You can ask yourself these questions as you read your composition:

Writing Checklist Questions

- ☐ Did I respond to the prompt?
- ☐ Is the main idea clear?
- ☐ Do the details all support the main idea?
- ☐ Did I make the best word choices?
- ☐ Is it all in a logical order?
- ☐ Are all my sentences complete?
- ☐ Are there any errors in usage, grammar, punctuation, and spelling?

Use Precise Words

As you write, read it back to yourself. Can readers tell what you mean? Can they picture what you describe? One way to help people picture what you are saying is to use **precise words**. These are words that describe clearly. Avoid vague words like *good*, *bad*, *stuff*, and *thing*.

Think back to the topic of having superpowers for a day. Here is the draft of one student's paper. Look at the underlined parts. Do you see how they might be confusing?

> One day, I woke up and had superpowers. I knew theyd last for just that day. My powers included flying, like Superman. I could just jump up and fly. I could also breathe under water, like Aquaman. My magic rope made people tell the truth, so they had to say what they did wrong. Wonder Woman <u>had one</u>. first, I called the police and told them <u>I could help</u>. By flyng fast, I caught some bank robbers that try to run away. Then, I put the rope around them and made them confess. The police put them in jail when I

> was done with them! Next there's innocent people on a bridge. Two guys took a truck and knocked cars into the river! I saved them by going underwater and flying the injured people to the hospital. The police were grateful, and people were happy I was around, even for just one day.

Now look at the revised draft. The writer is using more precise words. They help make the writing more clear.

> One day, I woke up and had superpowers. I knew theyd last for just that day. My powers included flying, like Superman. I could just jump up and fly. I could also breathe under water, like Aquaman. My magic rope made people tell the truth, so they had to say what they did wrong. Wonder Woman had a rope like that. first, I called the police and told them what I could do to help fight crime. By flyng fast, I caught some bank robbers that try to run away. Then, I put the rope around them and made them confess. The police put them in jail when I was done with them! Next there's innocent people on a bridge. Two thieves took a truck and knocked cars into the river! I saved the victims in the cars by going underwater and flying the injured people to the hospital. The police were grateful, and people were happy I was around, even for just one day.

Include Details

In addition to colorful words, there are other **details** you can include. They can make your writing more interesting. Supporting sentences tell details about your point. Supporting sentences have examples, facts, and stories. They give your reader more information. They give proof that what you are saying is right. They help you grab your reader's interest so he or she wants to read what you wrote.

Edit

When you **edit**, you find and fix small errors. This includes looking for and fixing errors in areas like these:

- spelling
- punctuation
- capitalization
- agreement
- verb tenses
- noun and pronoun forms
- conjunctions
- prepositions

Did you notice the errors in the superhero essay? Here you are, underlined.

One day, I woke up and had superpowers. I knew theyd last for just that day. My powers included flying, like Superman. I could just jump up and fly. I could also breathe under water, like Aquaman. My magic rope made people tell the truth, so they had to say what they did wrong. Wonder Woman had a rope like that. first, I called the police and told them what I could do to help fight crime. By flyng fast, I caught some bank robbers that try to run away. Then, I put the rope around them and made them confess. The police put them in jail when I was done with them! Next there's innocent people on a bridge. Two thieves took a truck and knocked cars into the river! I saved the victims in the cars by going underwater and flying the injured people to the hospital. The police were grateful, and people were happy I was around, even for just one day.

The first mistake needs an apostrophe. It should be "they'd."

The next one needs to be capitalized. "First" comes at the start of a sentence.

The word "flyng" should be spelled "flying."

Finally, "Next" is an introductory word. It needs a comma after it. And "there's" is short for "there is." But "innocent people" is plural. So it needs to say "Next, there were."

Practice 2: Revising Your Writing

W 1–5, 10 (DOK 3)

Go back to the compositions you drafted. Now do the activities below for each one.

1 Look at the draft for the first prompt, "Write a story about something that happened that made you very happy."

Revise your writing to make sure it's clear. Use the checklist on page 199.

Edit for errors. See chapters 7, 8, and 9 for details about what to look for.

2 Look at your draft for the second prompt, "Describe the thing that you would most like to have if you could buy anything."

Revise to make sure it's clear. Use the checklist on page 199.

Edit for errors. See chapters 7, 8, and 9 for details about what to look for.

Publish

When you are done revising and editing, you can **publish your writing**. This means you share the final version with others. You can type it on the computer. Then you can print it to give to your teacher or other students. You can also put a version of it online. If your class has a website, there may be a place to see student essays.

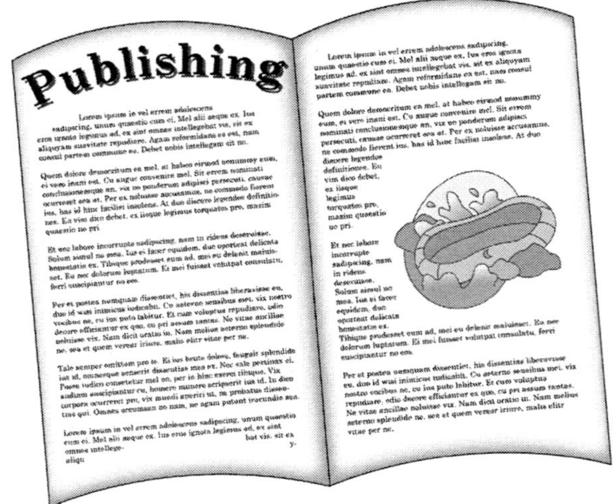

Publishing your work helps you to share with others. Then you can ask for help. Or you can work with a group to create new stories and improve each others' writing.

Activity

W 1.a–d, 2.a–d, 3.a–d, 4, 5, 6

Did you finish writing your essay about something that made you happy? How about the one about what you would most like to buy? Now it's time to publish them!

Take the first essay, and make a small book out of it. You can print it on paper that you can bind together with clips or yarn. Or you can make a book out of construction paper. Then write your story in it. You could also glue the printed pages inside. Add some pictures as visuals to help tell the story of what made you happy.

Take the second essay, and publish it to a webpage. Ask your teacher or tutor for help.

CHAPTER 12 SUMMARY

The **writing process** includes planning, drafting, and revising.

Step one is **planning**. First, you **select a topic**.

Next, you do some **prewriting**. This can include the following:

- You can **look up facts** and **use what you know**.
- **Brainstorming** means listing ideas about a topic.
- **Graphic organizers** can help ideas fit together.
- **Drafting** a composition means writing it out. It includes these steps:
- **Develop ideas** by picking one **main idea** and several **supporting details**. Add **examples** for each detail.

Put your ideas in a **logical order**. For a narrative, make sure that the **sequence of events** is clear.

Use **specific words** to help readers know what you mean.

Revising means improving your writing by making sure it is clear, complete, and well organized.

Editing is looking for and fixing small errors like punctuation and spelling mistakes.

Publishing is producing your final composition for others to read.

Chapter 12 Review

W 1–8, 10 (DOK 3)

For the chapter review in chapter 11, you picked a topic. Then you did some research about that topic. Take out your notes now. Use them to plan and write an essay. Here are the steps to take:

Plan and Draft

- [x] Select a topic.
- [ ] Develop ideas.
- [ ] Write a draft.

Revise

- [ ] Make sure ideas are clear.
- [ ] Add precise words and details.

Edit

- [ ] Fix any errors.

Publish

- [ ] Type your essay or report.
- [ ] Upload it for others to read.

Index

T

U

V

W

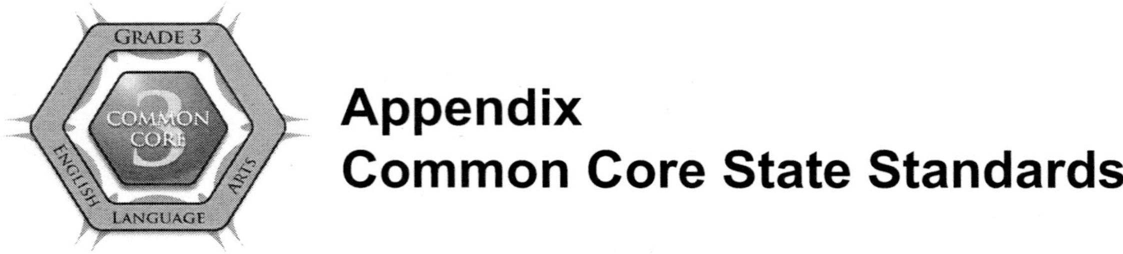

Appendix
Common Core State Standards

The following Common Core State Standards for grade 3 are covered in *Mastering the Common Core in Grade 3 English Language Arts.*

Common Core English Language Arts Standards for Grade 3

Reading Literature

Key Ideas and Details

1. Ask and answer questions to demonstrate understanding of a text, referring explicitly to the text as the basis for the answers.
2. Recount stories, including fables, folktales, and myths from diverse cultures; determine the central message, lesson, or moral and explain how it is conveyed through key details in the text.
3. Describe characters in a story (e.g., their traits, motivations, or feelings) and explain how their actions contribute to the sequence of events.

Craft and Structure

4. Determine the meaning of words and phrases as they are used in a text, distinguishing literal from nonliteral language.
5. Refer to parts of stories, dramas, and poems when writing or speaking about a text, using terms such as chapter, scene, and stanza; describe how each successive part builds on earlier sections.
6. Distinguish their own point of view from that of the narrator or those of the characters.

Integration of Knowledge and Ideas

7. Explain how specific aspects of a text's illustrations contribute to what is conveyed by the words in a story (e.g., create mood, emphasize aspects of a character or setting).
8. (Not applicable to literature)
9. Compare and contrast the themes, settings, and plots of stories written by the same author about the same or similar characters (e.g., in books from a series).

Range of Reading and Complexity of Text

10. By the end of the year, read and comprehend literature, including stories, dramas, and poetry, at the high end of the grades 2–3 text complexity band independently and proficiently.

Reading Informational Texts

Key Ideas and Details

1. Ask and answer questions to demonstrate understanding of a text, referring explicitly to the text as the basis for the answers.
2. Determine the main idea of a text; recount the key details and explain how they support the main idea.
3. Describe the relationship between a series of historical events, scientific ideas or concepts, or steps in technical procedures in a text, using language that pertains to time, sequence, and cause/effect.

Craft and Structure

4. Determine the meaning of general academic and domain-specific words and phrases in a text relevant to a *grade 3 topic or subject area.*
5. Use text features and search tools (e.g., key words, sidebars, hyperlinks) to locate information relevant to a given topic efficiently.
6. Distinguish their own point of view from that of the author of a text.

Integration of Knowledge and Ideas

7. Use information gained from illustrations (e.g., maps, photographs) and the words in a text to demonstrate understanding of the text (e.g., where, when, why, and how key events occur).
8. Describe the logical connection between particular sentences and paragraphs in a text (e.g., comparison, cause/effect, first/second/third in a sequence).
9. Compare and contrast the most important points and key details presented in two texts on the same topic.

Range of Reading and Level of Text Complexity

10. By the end of the year, read and comprehend informational texts, including history/social studies, science, and technical texts, at the high end of the grades 2–3 text complexity band independently and proficiently.

Reading: Foundational Skills

Phonics and Word Recognition

3. Know and apply grade-level phonics and word analysis skills in decoding words.
   a. Identify and know the meaning of the most common prefixes and derivational suffixes.
   b. Decode words with common Latin suffixes.
   c. Decode multi-syllable words.
   d. Read grade-appropriate irregularly spelled words.

Appendix

Fluency

4. Read with sufficient accuracy and fluency to support comprehension.
   a. Read grade-level text with purpose and understanding.
   b. Read grade-level prose and poetry orally with accuracy, appropriate rate, and expression.
   c. Use context to confirm or self-correct word recognition and understanding, rereading as necessary.

<u>Writing</u>

Text Types and Purposes

1. Write opinion pieces on topics or texts, supporting a point of view with reasons.
   a. Introduce the topic or text they are writing about, state an opinion, and create an organizational structure that lists reasons.
   b. Provide reasons that support the opinion.
   c. Use linking words and phrases (e.g., *because*, *therefore*, *since*, *for example*) to connect opinion and reasons.
   d. Provide a concluding statement or section.
2. Write informative/explanatory texts to examine a topic and convey ideas and information clearly.
   a. Introduce a topic and group related information together; include illustrations when useful to aiding comprehension.
   b. Develop the topic with facts, definitions, and details.
   c. Use linking words and phrases (e.g., *also*, *another*, *and*, *more*, *but*) to connect ideas within categories of information.
   d. Provide a concluding statement or section.
3. Write narratives to develop real or imagined experiences or events using effective technique, descriptive details, and clear event sequences.
   a. Establish a situation and introduce a narrator and/or characters; organize an event sequence that unfolds naturally.
   b. Use dialogue and descriptions of actions, thoughts, and feelings to develop experiences and events or show the response of characters to situations.
   c. Use temporal words and phrases to signal event order.
   d. Provide a sense of closure.

Production and Distribution of Writing

4. With guidance and support from adults, produce writing in which the development and organization are appropriate to task and purpose. (Grade-specific expectations for writing types are defined in standards 1–3 above.)
5. With guidance and support from peers and adults, develop and strengthen writing as needed by planning, revising, and editing.

6. With guidance and support from adults, use technology to produce and publish writing (using keyboarding skills) as well as to interact and collaborate with others.

Research to Build and Present Knowledge

7. Conduct short research projects that build knowledge about a topic.
8. Recall information from experiences or gather information from print and digital sources; take brief notes on sources and sort evidence into provided categories.
9. (Begins in grade 4)

Range of Writing

10. Write routinely over extended time frames (time for research, reflection, and revision) and shorter time frames (a single sitting or a day or two) for a range of discipline-specific tasks, purposes, and audiences.

Speaking and Listening

Comprehension and Collaboration

1. Engage effectively in a range of collaborative discussions (one-on-one, in groups, and teacher-led) with diverse partners on *grade 3 topics and texts,* building on others' ideas and expressing their own clearly.
   a. Come to discussions prepared, having read or studied required material; explicitly draw on that preparation and other information known about the topic to explore ideas under discussion.
   b. Follow agreed-upon rules for discussions (e.g., gaining the floor in respectful ways, listening to others with care, speaking one at a time about the topics and texts under discussion).
   c. Ask questions to check understanding of information presented, stay on topic, and link their comments to the remarks of others.
   d. Explain their own ideas and understanding in light of the discussion.
2. Determine the main ideas and supporting details of a text read aloud or information presented in diverse media and formats, including visually, quantitatively, and orally.
3. Ask and answer questions about information from a speaker, offering appropriate laboration and detail.

Presentation of Knowledge and Ideas

4. Report on a topic or text, tell a story, or recount an experience with appropriate facts and relevant, descriptive details, speaking clearly at an understandable pace.
5. Create engaging audio recordings of stories or poems that demonstrate fluid reading at an understandable pace; add visual displays when appropriate to emphasize or enhance certain facts or details.
6. Speak in complete sentences when appropriate to task and situation in order to provide requested detail or clarification.

Appendix

Language

Conventions of Standard English

1. Demonstrate command of the conventions of standard English grammar and usage when writing or speaking.
   a. Explain the function of nouns, pronouns, verbs, adjectives, and adverbs in general and their functions in particular sentences.
   b. Form and use regular and irregular plural nouns.
   c. Use abstract nouns (e.g., *childhood*).
   d. Form and use regular and irregular verbs.
   e. Form and use the simple (e.g., *I walked*; *I walk*; *I will walk*) verb tenses.
   f. Ensure subject-verb and pronoun-antecedent agreement.*
   g. Form and use comparative and superlative adjectives and adverbs, and choose between them depending on what is to be modified.
   h. Use coordinating and subordinating conjunctions.
   i. Produce simple, compound, and complex sentences.
2. Demonstrate command of the conventions of standard English capitalization, punctuation, and spelling when writing.
   a. Capitalize appropriate words in titles.
   b. Use commas in addresses.
   c. Use commas and quotation marks in dialogue.
   d. Form and use possessives.
   e. Use conventional spelling for high-frequency and other studied words and for adding suffixes to base words (e.g., *sitting*, *smiled*, *cries*, *happiness*).
   f. Use spelling patterns and generalizations (e.g., word families, position-based spellings, syllable patterns, ending rules, meaningful word parts) in writing words.
   g. Consult reference materials, including beginning dictionaries, as needed to check and correct spellings.

Knowledge of Language

3. Use knowledge of language and its conventions when writing, speaking, reading, or listening.
   a. Choose words and phrases for effect.*
   b. Recognize and observe differences between the conventions of spoken and written standard English.

Vocabulary Acquisition and Use

4. Determine or clarify the meaning of unknown and multiple-meaning word and phrases based on grade 3 reading and content, choosing flexibly from a range of strategies.
   a. Use sentence-level context as a clue to the meaning of a word or phrase.
   b. Determine the meaning of the new word formed when a known affix is added to a known word (e.g., *agreeable/disagreeable*, *comfortable/uncomfortable*, *care/careless*, *heat/preheat*).
   c. Use a known root word as a clue to the meaning of an unknown word with the same root (e.g., *company*, *companion*).
   d. Use glossaries or beginning dictionaries, both print and digital, to determine or clarify the precise meaning of key words and phrases.
5. Demonstrate understanding of figurative language, word relationships and nuances in word meanings.
   a. Distinguish the literal and nonliteral meanings of words and phrases in context (e.g., *take steps*).
   b. Identify real-life connections between words and their use (e.g., describe people who are *friendly* or *helpful*).
   c. Distinguish shades of meaning among related words that describe states of mind or degrees of certainty (e.g., *knew*, *believed*, *suspected*, *heard*, *wondered*).
6. Acquire and use accurately grade-appropriate conversational, general academic, and domain-specific words and phrases, including those that signal spatial and temporal relationships (e.g., *After dinner that night we went looking for them*).

[Note: Beginning in grade 3, skills and understandings that are particularly likely to require continued attention in higher grades as they are applied to increasingly sophisticated writing and speaking are marked with an asterisk (*).]